# UNIQUE Washington

## A Guide to the State's Quirks, Charisma, and Character

*Tom Barr*

John Muir Publications
Santa Fe, New Mexico

**Special thanks** to Bill Palmroth; Allen Edwards, USDA Forest Service; Walter Bronowitz; Mark Cedergreen, Westport Charters; Bellingham-Whatcom Co. Convention & Visitors Bureau; The Boeing Company and Boeing Company Archives; Centrum Productions; Chateau Ste. Michelle Winery; Clarkston Chamber of Commerce; Columbia River Gorge National Scenic Area; Everett Public Library; East King County Convention & Visitor's Bureau; Ephrata Chamber of Commerce; Greater Othello Chamber of Commerce; Greater Vancouver Chamber of Commerce; Lake Chelan Chamber of Commerce; Long Beach Peninsula Visitor's Bureau; Lynden Chamber of Commerce; Makah Cultural and Research Center; Microsoft Corporation; Mount Rainier National Park; National Forest Service/National Park Service Outdoor Recreation Information Center; North Cascades National Park; North Olympic Peninsula Visitor & Convention Bureau; Ocean Shores Development Association; Odessa Economic Development Council; Okanogan Chamber of Commerce; Olympic National Park; Port Angeles Chamber of Commerce; Port Townsend Chamber of Commerce; Roosevelt Recreational Enterprises; San Juan Island National Historical Park; Seattle Arts Commission; Seattle King County News Bureau; Spokane Regional Convention & Visitors Bureau; Tacoma-Pierce County Visitor and Convention Bureau; Tri-Cities Visitor & Convention Bureau; Twin Cities Chamber of Commerce; U.S. Fish and Wildlife Service; Washington Apple Commission; Washington Department of Fish and Wildlife; Washington State Convention and Trade Center; Washington State Department of Trade and Economic Development; Washington State University Special Collections; Washington Wine Commission; Wenatchee Area Visitor & Convention Bureau; Westport/Grayland Chamber of Commerce; Whitman College Special Collections; Whitman Mission National Historic Site; Yakima Valley Museum; Yakima Valley Visitors and Convention Bureau.

John Muir Publications, P. O. Box 613, Santa Fe, NM 87504

First edition. First printing February 1995

Library of Congress Cataloging-in-Publication Data
Barr, Tom.
Unique Washington : a guide to the state's quirks, charisma, and character/
Tom Barr—1st ed.
   p.  cm.
   Includes index.
   ISBN 1-56261-192-5 : $10.95
1. Washington (State)—Guidebooks.   I. Title
F889.3.B36 1995                94-23407
917.9704'43—dc20                   CIP

**Production:** Kathryn Lloyd-Strongin, Sarah Johansson
**Editorial:** Elizabeth Wolf, Dianna Delling, Jo Ann Baldinger
**Design:** Ken Wilson
**Typesetting:** Go West Graphics
**Illustrations:** Bette Brodsky
**Cover Photo:** Leo de Wys Inc./Steve Vidler
**Cover Photo Inset:** Leo de Wys Inc./Richard Sipa
**Back Cover Photo:** Bellingham Convention and Visitors Bureau

Distributed to the book trade by
Publishers Group West
Emeryville, California

# CONTENTS

# INTRODUCTION

Nothing but emerald-green forests, snow-capped mountains, rushing rivers, and blue skies. That's Washington, right? Climb Mount Rainier, sail through the San Juan Islands, spend an afternoon on a Washington State Ferry, and backpack into the rugged wilderness of the North Cascades, and you know you couldn't be anywhere except the Evergreen State. Cross the Cascade Mountains and you'll find a Washington that was once barren desert, transformed by irrigation into some of the earth's most productive agricultural lands.

Mount Rainier National Park

*Mount Rainier's snow-capped peak, mirror-smooth lakes, and lush forest are characteristic of western Washington's scenery*

Of course, there are still many things to discover about unique Washington. Did you know that National Forest and Park lands cover over one-third of Washington, or that it has over 1,700 lakes and more than 3,000 miles of shoreline? Did you know that in Washington you can scuba dive and beachcomb in the morning and ski the high country in the afternoon, sailboard in the Columbia River Gorge, and climb Mount St. Helens' crater? Or that Washington festivals celebrate everything from Bigfoot, irrigation, and rain to rodeos and Native American and ethnic heritages?

*Unique Washington* presents fascinating facts, intriguing destinations, tantalizing trivia, handy charts, and quick access maps in a user-friendly format. Where else can you find recipes for healthful Northwest cuisine and sumptuous seafood, the best places to see bluebirds and watch wildlife, and tips for off-the-beaten-path recreation? However you choose to use this book, you'll soon find out what is unique about Washington State.

## Busy Border

More people cross the Canadian–U.S. border at Blaine's **Peace Arch** than at any other place in Washington. The six-story-high arch on Interstate 5 has one massive column in each country, testifying to almost two centuries of peace between the two nations. It was the first structure of its kind in the world and was built with volunteer labor from both countries. Surrounding parks were built with donations from thousands of American and Canadian school children, limited to a maximum of ten cents each. The commemorative inscription from the 1921 dedication reads: "Open for 100 years of peaceful relations and may these gates never be closed." "Children of a Common Mother" is inscribed across the arch on the American side, and "Brethren Dwelling Together in Peace" faces Canada. Plaques depict the American *Mayflower* and the Canadian fur trading ship, *Beaver*. At the annual Peace Arch celebration on the second Sunday in June, 10,000 people exchange flags and other symbols of friendship. *FYI:* Peach Arch State Park; 360-332-8221.

Merchandise totalling $400, based on fair retail value in the country where purchased, may be entered duty-free subject to certain regulations. Two U.S. Customs Service booklets, *Know Before You Go* and *Customs Hints*, are available at most Washington visitors centers. They provide information on clearing customs, exemptions, and prohibited and restricted articles.

## Washington

Population:
4,866,663

Area:
66,582 sq. miles

State Capital:
Olympia

Nickname:
Evergreen State

Date of Statehood:
November 11, 1889

Highest Elevation:
Mount Rainier
14,411 ft.

State Tree:
Western hemlock

State Bird:
Willow goldfinch

State Animal:
Roosevelt elk

State Gem:
Petrified wood

# THEN AND NOW

## 23,000 B.C.–A.D. 1592

People began crossing the Bering Land Bridge from Asia to North America approximately 25,000 years ago. By 12,000 years ago, their descendants had migrated into what is now Washington, where they found Ice Age glaciers covering the northern third of the state. Until about 8,000 B.C. they lived by killing mastodons, mammoths, prehistoric bison, and primitive horses. By 8,000 B.C., after the big game animals died out, hunters settled down to live on food provided during the growing seasons.

Then, as now, the Cascade Mountains formed a great north-to-south barrier across Washington. By stopping the moisture-laden Pacific Ocean winds, the mountains divided the land into wet and dry climates and, except along the Columbia River lowlands, inhibited cultural interaction. The floras and faunas of the wet and arid regions ultimately led to unique Native American cultures.

Near the coast, rivers teemed with fish. Forests provided deer, elk, and other game. Coastal Indians hunted, fished, and had leisure time to develop large permanent villages with intricate social structures. They became sophisticated artisans and proficient woodworkers who constructed large ocean-going canoes and huge plank houses.

In eastern Washington, villages of small pit houses and mat lodges clustered along river banks. Although eastern Washington Indians fished for salmon on the Columbia and Snake Rivers, they also made seasonal migrations to hunt and collect roots and berries. By 6,500 years ago, they had developed large villages, extensive trade networks, and complex mythologies.

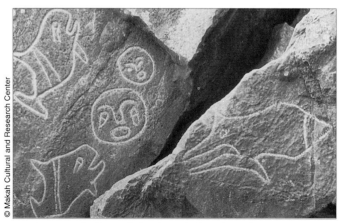

© Makah Cultural and Research Center

*Ancient petroglyphs made by the Makah Indians decorate rocks on the northern Washington coast*

Evidence of these paleo-Indians has been found throughout the state in archaeological sites and petroglyphs. On the Olympic Peninsula near the community of Sequim (pronounced "squim"), archaeologists discovered an 11,850-year-old mastodon tusk and a weapon made of animal bones. A Wenatchee orchard yielded the largest paleo-Indian Clovis points. The 12,500-year-old points are over $8^{1}/_{2}$ inches long.

Ten thousand years ago, prehistoric Indians spent their winters at the **Marmes Rock Shelter** in southeast Washington. Excavations have produced burial and cultural materials in eight geological strata. Although the site was inundated by the backwaters of Monumental Dam, a two-mile trail leads from **Lyons Ferry State Park** to a bluff overlooking the cliff shelter. *FYI:* 509-646-3252.

Washington's best-preserved archaeological site is **Ozette**, near the Olympic Peninsula's Neah Bay. The village was occupied for at least 2,000 years. Approximately 300 years ago it was buried by a mud slide, which preserved homes and their contents.

Among the artifacts are planks covered with whale-figure carvings and a wooden carving of a whale fin inlaid with hundreds of sea-otter teeth. The **Makah Cultural and Research Center Museum** displays many artifacts, along with a full-scale replica of a 15th-century Indian long house. *FYI:* Makah Cultural Center, Neah Bay; 360-645-2711.

**Horsethief Lake State Park**, near Wishram on the Columbia River, was an Indian trading ground centuries ago. You can take a five-minute walk from the parking lot to original petroglyphs. Wakemap Mound, an island near the park, has yielded 2,000-year-old artifacts. *FYI:* Horsethief Lake State Park; 509-767-1159.

## Early Explorations: 1592–1792

A Greek sea captain, Apostolos Valerianos, operating under the alias of Juan de Fuca, may or may not have been the first explorer to see Washington's coastline. The way Valerianos (de Fuca) told it, while employed by Spain in 1592 he had sailed up the Pacific Coast to a latitude of 47 degrees. There he found a passage situated below a "great headland or island rich in gold, silver, and pearls." After spending 20 days exploring, de Fuca said he sailed out of the strait and right into the Atlantic Ocean!

No one believed him, although at the time North America was thought to be a very thin continent and de Fuca's descriptions of the entrance, natives, and landscape were accurate. Nearly 200 years passed before sea captains William Barkley and John Meares saw the strait Juan de Fuca had described. It separates Washington from Vancouver Island and is named in his honor.

## Cook and Vancouver

Captain James Cook of the British Royal Navy sailed up the coast in 1778 on a scientific expedition to find the Northwest Passage. Thanks to bad weather he missed both the Columbia River and the Strait of Juan de Fuca. While Cook's ships were refitted on Vancouver Island, his crew traded trinkets for furs. After

*Captain George Vancouver named Mount Baker, above, and more than 40 other sites*

Tom Barr

Cook was killed by Hawaiian natives, his crew continued to China and sold the furs for exorbitant prices. Their reports sparked the first Northwest fur trade.

In 1791 Captain George Vancouver came to chart the coast and seek the Northwest Passage. After mapping the coast and Puget Sound, he landed near the present city of Everett on June 4, 1792, and claimed the land for England. He called it New Georgia.

## Russia, Spain Come Calling

Several other nations also set sail for the Northwest. In 1728 and 1741, Vitus Bering made two expeditions to Alaska on behalf of Russia. Although he never reached Washington, Russia considered his voyages as legitimizing its claim to the entire Pacific Northwest. Worried by Russia's advancement, Spain launched several expeditions in the mid-1770s. The first landings on Washington soil were made by Bruno de Heceta at Point Granville and by Juan Francisco de la Bodega y Quadra near the Hoh River, where his party was killed by Indians. These men established Spain's claim to the Pacific Northwest.

Spain founded a settlement at Neah Bay in 1792. Because of the bay's lack of protection from storms and its rocky bottom, it was abandoned five months later.

### Naming Names

Many western Washington landmarks were named by early explorers. Captain Cook named Cape Flattery because, according to his logs, "it had flattered [deceived] us with hopes of finding a harbor." Captain George Vancouver was the biggest name-dropper. He named Port Townsend for an English nobleman, and Mount Rainier and Hood Canal for British admirals. Puget Sound honored Vancouver's lieutenant, Peter Puget, and Whidbey Island was given the name of its discoverer, Joseph Whidbey. Vancouver also named Mount Baker, Vashon Island, Port Orchard, Deception Pass, and more than 40 other sites. Captain John Meares named Mount Olympus, Cape Disappointment, Shoalwater Bay, and Tatoosh Island.

## Under Four Flags

At the end of the 18th century everyone, it seemed, claimed the Pacific Northwest. No one actually owned it. A Joint Occupancy Treaty signed in 1818 by England and the United States gave both nations rights to occupy and use the Pacific Northwest but denied them possession of it. Because it was too expensive to keep other nations out, and the Northwest's forests left little room for agriculture, Spain lost interest by 1793 but retained its claims until 1819. Russia relinquished its claims in 1824.

Robert Esposito

*An operating replica of Captain Robert Gray's* Lady Washington *is the centerpiece of Grays Harbor Historical Seaport*

### Captain Robert Gray

On May 11, 1792, Captain Robert Gray, a Boston trader, discovered the Columbia River and named it after his ship. Crossing the bar, he anchored near today's Ilwaco, Washington, and traded with Indians for sea otters and beaver pelts.

The discovery was only one of his many accomplishments. Gray was the first American to sail around Cape Horn and into the Hawaiian Islands, and to circumnavigate the earth. He was also the first American to land in Oregon and Washington and to start a United States fur trading business.

Although Gray's discovery of the Columbia River established America's claim to the Pacific Northwest, he did not feel it was particularly significant. Neither, apparently, did the United States. When Gray's widow petitioned Congress for a pension or an Oregon land grant, her request was denied.

Monterey Bay Aquarium

*The Washington maritime fur trade targeted sea otters*

## Sea Otters

A thriving maritime fur trade targeted sea otters. While Indians prized the black-brown pelts stippled with silver, they gladly traded them for metal tools, utensils, and beads. One chisel bought 200 skins. In 1785, 600 pelts sold in China for $20,000 and the prices skyrocketed for several years. By the 20th century, sea otters, which once numbered in the millions, were virtually extinct. Protection programs have brought them back to a population of over 35,000. Sea otters are unique among marine mammals in that for body warmth they depend entirely on an insulating blanket of air trapped in their dense fur coats.

## Lewis and Clark

The Lewis and Clark expedition of 1805 strengthened America's claim to the Pacific Northwest. While following the Snake and Columbia Rivers through southern Washington, the expedition spent two days at the confluence of the rivers at what is now **Sacajawea State Park**. Interpretive center exhibits about their journey feature outstanding collections of arrowheads found at the ancient Indian meeting place. *FYI:* Road 40 East, Pasco; 509-545-2361.

En route to the Pacific, they zig-zagged between the Columbia's Washington and Oregon shorelines while enduring cold, hunger, and drenching rain. On November 7, 1805 Clark's journal entry read: "Ocian [sic] in view! O! The joy!" A roadside marker and wooden statue on U.S. 101 pinpoint their campsite. Nearby, **Fort Canby State Park's** Interpretive Center tracks the expedition's journey from planning stages to the Columbia River with murals, photographs, and original journal entries. *FYI:* Long Beach Peninsula; 360-642-3078.

## Fur Forts

After 1792 the fur trade became a land operation centered on beaver. The overland fur trade fired fierce competition between England's Hudson's Bay Company, the British-French Canadian North West Company, and America's Pacific Fur Company.

The North West Company established the first non-Indian settlement in eastern Washington when it built Spokane House trading post in 1810, nine miles north of present-day Spokane. John Jacob Astor followed with the Pacific Fur Company at Astoria, Oregon, and in 1811 built Fort Okanogan, the first American post in Washington. Explorer-trader David Thompson raced down the Columbia River to solidify North West Company claims and thus became the first to explore the Columbia from source to mouth.

The next year Astor's company built Fort Spokane within a few yards of Spokane House. Nothing remains of the two Spokane posts, and the Okanogan fort site is covered by Wells Dam backwaters. Nearby, **Fort Okanogan Interpretive Center** contains historic sign-boards and other displays. *FYI:* Star Route, Pateros; 509-923-2473.

During the War of 1812 the Americans feared a British takeover and sold all their forts, trading posts, and furs to the North West Company for $58,291. After their departure, the North West Company continued to operate Fort Okanogan and other American posts. An 1814 treaty between England and the United States stipulated the return of all territory seized by both sides during the War of 1812.

In 1821, when the British government forced a merger of the Hudson's Bay and North West Companies, it gave the Hudson's Bay Company a virtual 25-year monopoly on the Columbia fur trade. The company was a fixture in Washington until 1860.

## Hudson's Bay Company Forts

Fort Vancouver, built in 1825, was the hub of the Pacific Northwest. Its chief agent, Dr. John McLoughlin, ruled over everything from northern California to Alaska and from the Pacific to the Rocky Mountains. Washington's entertainment, agriculture, and industry originated at Fort Vancouver, site of the Northwest's first theatrical performance, sawmill, and gristmill. Its farms raised the region's first peas, oats, barley, and wheat, and its orchards grew the first apples, pears, peaches, plums, and cherries. Fort Vancouver also had the first herds of cattle, horses, hogs, sheep, and goats.

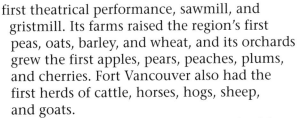

The stockade and five major buildings have been reconstructed on the original ground as **Fort Vancouver National Historic Site**. Artifacts excavated at the site are displayed in the visitor center and buildings. *FYI:* 612 East Reserve Street, Vancouver; 360-696-7655.

In 1833, the Hudson's Bay Company established Fort Nisqually near the southern tip of Puget Sound. Tacoma's **Point Defiance Park** contains a full-sized replica. The original house and granary are the the oldest standing structures in the state and are on the National Historic Register. *FYI:* 206-591-5339.

Events
**Fort Vancouver Brigade Encampment:** During July, participants dress in circa 1840 costumes, camp in teepees, and demonstrate skills reminiscent of brigade encampments at the original fort.
**Fort Vancouver Candlelight Tours:** The October event recreates a typical 1845 evening at the fort.

## Whitman Mission

In 1836, hoping to convert Indians to Christianity, Marcus and Narcissa Whitman established a mission near Walla Walla. Their daughter, Alice Clarissa Whitman, was the first child born of American parents in Washington. By 1843 the mission had become an important stop on the Oregon Trail. When measles carried by emigrants killed half the Cayuse tribe, many Indians believed they were being exterminated to make room for white settlers. On November 29, l847, the Cayuse attacked, killing the Whitmans and 12 other people, and taking 50 hostages.

*Marcus Whitman*

Whitman Mission National Historic Site

At **Whitman Mission National Historic Site**, trails lead from the visitor center to the mission site, graves, and a monument that stands atop a hill overlooking the Walla Walla Valley. *FYI:* R2, Walla Walla; 509-522-6360.

## Oregon and Washington Territories

By 1846 the United States had acquired sole possession of Washington and Oregon. Two years later, President James Polk signed a bill creating the Oregon Territory. It included the present states of Oregon, Washington, and Idaho, and parts of Montana and Wyoming. When the huge land mass proved cumbersome to govern, the Washington Territory was created in 1853 and extended into northern Idaho and western Montana. Although local citizens requested the name Columbia Territory, Congress changed it to Washington.

*John R. Jackson's cabin, built in 1845, served as a home, general store, and courthouse*

## Early Settlements

Tumwater, Washington, founded in 1845, was the first Euro-American village north of the Columbia River. The early 1850s saw farming communities come to Whidbey Island and marked the start of Port Gamble, Seattle, Tacoma, Olympia, Centralia, and Oysterville on the Long Beach Peninsula. Sawmills were among the first industries. Centralia's blockhouse and founder's home were built in 1857 and are preserved in **Borst Park.** *FYI:* Southwest corner of I-5 Exit 82; 360-736-7687.

## Indian Wars and Treaty Troubles

Territorial Governor Isaac Stevens persuaded Washington's Indians to surrender their lands by 1855, but ratification of the treaties was postponed until 1859. From 1855 to 1858 there were many skirmishes between Indians, settlers, and the Army. The Army won several engagements and avoided others by retreating at night. In other engagements they broke the Indians' will to fight by rounding up and killing as many as 800 of their horses. In 1896 when prospectors overran part of the Colville Reservation, the federal government simply reduced the reservation's size, thus giving miners access to once-protected treaty lands.

### Fort Simcoe State Park

This 1856–59 infantry post is situated on a historically important Yakima Indian gathering spot. It exhibits several original furnished Victorian-style officers' homes, an original blockhouse, and reconstructed buildings. *FYI:* 30 miles west of Toppenish, Hwy. 220; 509-874-2372.

*Fort Simcoe exhibits original buildings and artifacts used at the post*

## Pig War

The Oregon Treaty of 1846 gave the United States undisputed possession of Washington but left unclear who owned San Juan Island. According to the treaty, the boundary "extended to the middle of the channel which separates the continent from Vancouver's Island." Unfortunately, there were two channels, and San Juan Island lay between them.

On June 15, 1859, American settler Lyman Cutlar killed a Hudson's Bay Company pig snacking in his San Juan Island potato patch and touched off an international incident. When Britain threatened to arrest Cutlar, Americans requested military protection. American troops commanded by Captain George Pickett (of future Gettysburg fame) were the first ashore. Soon 400 infantry, with a dozen cannons and an earthen wall, were looking at five British warships with 167 guns and over 2,100 sailors and Royal Marines. Token forces from both nations occupied the island for the next 12 years. The conflict was referred to Kaiser Wilhelm I of Germany for resolution. He ruled that the United States owned San Juan Island, thus establishing the final boundary between America and Canada. Today, the American and British camps comprise **San Juan Island National Historic Park**. Along with historical interpretation, the park offers shoreline and mountain hikes, beach activities, and bird-watching opportunities. *FYI:* American Camp, six miles south of Friday Harbor; English Camp, ten miles northwest of Friday Harbor; 360-378-2240.

## Prosperity Rules

*Puget Sound waterfronts did a bustling business in the 1800s shipping Washington timber*

Everett Public Library

In general, Washington rode out its territorial days on a wave of growth and prosperity punctuated by short-term booms and the rise of major industries. The Pacific Northwest's first salmon cannery opened in 1866, and Washington's first quartz lode was discovered in 1871. The years 1860 to l890 saw lumbering jump 40 percent and the beginning of pulp and paper mills. While farming remained the main occupation, stock-raising developed rapidly in eastern Washington.

The late 1880s also brought small range-wars between sheep and cattle ranchers. The severe winters of 1889 and 1890 devastated livestock herds but eased tensions as many ranchers turned to farming.

*Library of Congress*

## Tough Tunnels

Constructing railroad tunnels through the Cascade Mountains was a massive undertaking which gener-

*The "greatest raft ever built"—6,500 logs, each 125 feet long—floats down the Columbia River, a testament to Washington's powerful timber industry*

ated heated rivalries among work crews. In 1888, while breaking through the last few feet of rock in Stampede Tunnel, the west side foreman started squeezing through the small opening and met the east side representative. Supporters of both men rushed in and began pushing their respective foremen through the tunnel, battering and bloodying both men.

## Statehood Comes Collect

On November 11, 1889, Washington, with a population of 357,230, was admitted into the Union as the 42nd state. Montana, North Dakota, and South Dakota became states on this date as well. Federal officials telegraphed the news to Washington's territorial leaders in Olympia. But before they could receive the message, they had to pay for the telegram. It had been sent collect.

By 1912 the timber products industry was employing two-thirds of the state's wage earners

*Library of Congress*

## Statehood

In the century since statehood, events of epic proportions transformed Washington's landscape, shaped its economy, repositioned its place in international trade, and introduced sophisticated technology to warfare, transportation, and communication.

In 1905 Washington became the leading lumbering state and remained the prime timber producer until 1938. By 1912 the timber products industry was employing two-thirds of the state's wage earners. To insure future supplies, in 1941 Weyerhaeuser Corporation opened the first tree farm at Montesano. **The Forks Timber Museum** displays cover early pioneer life, agriculture, and logging. *FYI:* U.S. 101; 360-374-9663. **Pope and Talbot Historical Museum** chronicles the Northwest lumber industry. *FYI:* Port Gamble; 360-297-3341.

## Gateway to Alaska

On July 17, 1897, the steamer *Portland* entered Seattle's harbor carrying $800,000 in gold from the Yukon. Newspapers heralded the cargo as "a ton of gold" and sparked the last great gold rush. Seattle, the closest port, became the main supply base and exploded with new docks, shops, warehouses, and manufacturing plants. Merchants and shippers prospered, and eastern Washington farmers found a new market for their products. **Klondike Gold Rush National Historic Park** interprets this period with films, exhibits, and gold-panning demonstrations. *FYI:* 117 S. Main St., Seattle; 206-442-7220.

## Building a Better Plane

After taking his first plane ride in 1915, William Boeing decided he could build a better airplane. The first Boeing plane was powered by a 125-horsepower engine and flew 75 miles an hour for 320 miles before refueling.

In the 1990s, more than 80 percent of Boeing's business comes from commercial aircraft. With revenues of over $30 billion, in 1992 Boeing was the nation's largest aerospace firm, number-one exporter, and 12th largest industrial corporation. The company employs over 129,000 people worldwide. The **Boeing Everett Tour Center** offers 1½-hour tours of the Everett 747/767 plant (no children under ten, no photography or video cameras). *FYI:* Everett. From Interstate 5 Exit 189, three miles west on Hwy. 526; 206-342-4801.

*William Boeing (right) and pilot Eddie Hubbard at Lake Union for the first International Air Mail flight, March 3, 1919, from Vancouver, British Columbia, to Seattle*

Boeing's original manufacturing plant, called the Red Barn, is part of the **Museum of Flight** where over 50 full-sized aircraft—from a flying replica of Boeing's first plane to the Apollo spacecraft—are displayed. *FYI:* Seattle, I-5 Exit 158. 9404 East Marginal Way South; 206-764-5720.

## Damming the Columbia

With the construction of Grand Coulee Dam, a large irrigation system capable of providing water for central Washington's rich lands became a reality. More than 22 million cubic feet of soil and rock were removed to build Grand Coulee. Indian cemeteries, 12 towns, and over 3,000 people were relocated to make way for the dam and 150-mile-long Roosevelt Lake. When completed in 1941, the 4,173-foot structure's 1,650-foot spillway created a waterfall twice as high as Niagara. The dam's 11 million cubic yards of concrete are enough to build a six-lane highway around the nation. A visitor center offers exhibits and the world's largest laser light show. *FYI:* Grand Coulee; 509-633-9441.

*During World War II the Boeing Company and Puget Sound Shipyards were busy producing naval ships and military aircraft, including the famous B-17 bombers*

# Armed Forces

Washington's affiliation with the military started in the 1890s, when real estate developer William Bremer persuaded the government to locate a navy yard near his new town. At the **Bremerton Naval Museum**, photos, naval artifacts, and models illustrate the Puget Sound Naval Shipyards' history. *FYI:* 130 Washington Ave.; 360-479-SHIP.

During World War I, Camp Lewis was the largest cantonment in the United States. **Fort Lewis Military Museum** features Northwestern military history from 1803 to the present. *FYI:* I-5 Exit 120; 206-967-7206. **McChord Air Museum**, nearby, displays military aircraft and models, uniforms, and equipment. *FYI:* I-5 Exit 125; 206-984-2485.

Whidbey Island Naval Air Station was established in 1942 to guard the Kitsap Peninsula and Washington coast. **Forts Casey**, **Flagler**, and **Worden**, built between 1897 and 1911, were reactivated to form a "Triangle of Fire" to protect Puget Sound. **Forts Canby** and **Columbia** served similar functions on the Columbia River. The five forts are preserved as state parks. Attractions range from bunkers and 1900s buildings to campgrounds and shoreline hikes. *FYI:* Fort Casey, Hwy. 20, Coupeville, 360-678-4519; Fort Flagler, 8 miles northeast of Hadlock, 360-385-1259; Fort Worden, Port Townsend, 360-385-4730; Fort Canby, Ilwaco, 360-642-3078; Fort Columbia, 2 miles southeast of Chinook, Hwy 101, 360-777-8221.

## Hanford

In January 1943 the U.S. government and the DuPont Company bought more than 600 square miles of land along the Columbia River in central Washington and built the Hanford Atomic Works. At its peak, Hanford employed about 45,000 people and produced plutonium for atomic weapons. The atomic bomb that was dropped on Nagasaki, Japan, on August 9, 1945, contained Hanford plutonium. Although the last reactor closed in 1988, Hanford remains an important research center. **Hanford Science Center** interprets its history with interactive and environmental exhibits. *FYI:* 825 Jadwin Ave., Richland; 509-376-6374.

The **Fast Flux Test Facility (FFTF)** visitor center offers displays, models, and audio-visual presentations of the world's most advanced test reactor. *FYI:* 11 miles north of Richland; 509-376-6374.

## Bill Gates and Microsoft

Microsoft Corporation/Kathleen King

*Bill Gates*

Bill Gates started programming computers at age 13. In 1974, while a Harvard undergraduate, he developed BASIC, the first computer language program for a personal computer. Gates and his partner, Paul Allen, formed Microsoft Corporation. It grew from three employees in 1975 to 14,500 employees in 27 countries and net revenues of $3.8 billion in 1993. Based in Redmond, Microsoft is the world's leading manufacturer of personal computer software. Among its innovations are the Microsoft Mouse, Windows, and multimedia technology.

### Prominent Washingtonians

**Bing Crosby:** The famous singer/actor was born near Tacoma and graduated from Gonzaga University.

**Justice William O. Douglas:** The former Yakima resident held the longest term of any Supreme Court Justice, with 36 years on the bench.

**Henry "Scoop" Jackson:** Called "the best president we never had," he served six terms as a congressman and five terms as a state senator.

**Edward R. Murrow:** Raised in Skagit County, he is considered the father of television news.

## Washington Firsts and Inventions

In 1944 Washington became the first state to establish a policy and board to end job discrimination. MS-DOS was created in 1978 by Tim Paterson, a Seattle Computer Products programmer. In 1986 Seattle's Aldus Corporation developed PageMaker, the first practical desktop publishing program.

# THE NATURAL WORLD

Olympic National Park

*Olympic National Park's mountains contain six major glaciers*

## Building the Earth

Washington came together in bits and pieces, forged and welded by colliding tectonic plates, volcanism, uplifting, glacial scouring, and erosion. The moving, shifting, and shaking produced a state which contains virtually every known land feature in the United States.

Around a billion years ago the North American continent cracked and split, roughly along the line of Washington's eastern border. For the next 800 million years America's West Coast lay in eastern Washington. When the Pacific Ocean floor collided with North America and slid under the continent, friction melted the continental crust, creating gigantic lava flows that crystallized beneath the water's surface. As the ocean receded, the exposed rocks became part of northeastern Washington.

## Moving and Shaking

From 100 million to 50 million years ago, several large islands in the Pacific were fused to the mainland, forming the Okanogan Highlands and the Cascade Mountains. Volcanoes continued covering the land with lava for about 25 million years.

About 35 million years ago, subterranean forces began pushing up the Pacific Ocean floor. In southwestern Washington the sea floor was raised approximately two miles higher than most of the world's ocean crust, creating the Wallapa Hills. During the same period the Olympic Mountains were stuffed into a trench, then pushed and floated upward.

When volcanic activity ceased in the Cascades for 10 to 15 million years, a lengthy series of eruptions in southeastern Washington created the Columbia Plateau. Afterwards renewed volcanism in the Cascades started building most of the big volcanoes that dominate Washington's skyline today. They include Mount Baker, 10,750 feet; Mount Adams, 12,307 ft.; and Mount Rainier, 14,411 feet. Rainier reached its maximum height about 75,000 years ago. During this time volcanic ash and dust blew across the Columbia Plateau to cover the Palouse Hills.

A series of Ice Ages began between 2 and 3 million years ago, covering most of the northern third of Washington plus all the higher mountains. Puget Sound and the Okanogan Valley were eroded by ice, and gigantic floods rerouted the Columbia River and scoured the Columbia Plateau.

## National Parks and Monuments

### Olympic National Park

The park's 908,720 acres occupy most of the Olympic Peninsula. It encompasses glaciers, mountains, wildflower meadows, alpine lakes, rain forests, hot springs, Pacific surf, and wilderness beaches. No other national park provides refuge for such diverse animals as Roosevelt elk

Olympic National Park

*Olympic National Park's 57 miles of primitive coastline reward beach-lovers with magnificent scenery, tide pools, and dramatic sunsets*

(the park is home to the world's largest herd), whales, seals, bears, mountain lions, and over 140 species of birds.

The Hoh, Queets, and Quinault Valleys, with their eerie yellow-green glow, are the finest examples of temperate rain forests in the U.S. Here Sitka spruce, western hemlock, western red cedar, and Douglas fir grow to record sizes, reaching heights of 300 feet and 23 feet in circumferences. Mount Olympus, the park's highest point at 7,965 feet, is the nation's wettest spot. It receives 200 inches of annual precipitation.

Most of the park is roadless, but crisscrossed with hiking trails. Boating, river rafting, horse packing, cross-country skiing, snowshoeing, fishing, mountain climbing, camping, and wildlife viewing are popular activities. *FYI:* 600 East Park Ave., Port Angeles; 360-452-4501.

### Mount Rainier National Park

This isolated cone towers over 9,000 feet above the ridges of the surrounding Cascade Mountains. On clear days the gleaming white landmark is visible for hundreds of miles in all directions. Ranier is a mountain of many moods with dazzling wildflower meadows, huge snowfields, rugged glaciers, and dense forests of western hemlock, Douglas fir, and western red cedar. The 235,612-acre park is etched with canyons, ice caves, lakes, rivers, and waterfalls.

*In 1920 a group of climbers paused to fly the American flag atop Mount Rainier*

Mount Rainier National Park Collection

At 14,411 feet, Mount Rainier is Washington's highest peak. With 41 glaciers spread over 40 square miles, it has the largest single-peak glacial system in the continental United States. Because of its height, Rainier in effect makes its own weather. Storms materialize suddenly even in summer. In 1972, the world records for annual snowfall (93 feet) and snowfall in a single month (25.5 feet) were set at Rainier.

The park is famous for its wildflower meadows and is home to over 130 species of birds and 50 mammals. It offers scenic drives, climbing, snowshoeing, and cross-country skiing. Some 300 miles of trails are usually snow-free from mid-July through September. With the exception of 18 miles of road between the southwest entrance and Paradise Visitor Center, all roads close in winter. *FYI:* Mount Rainier National Park, Ashford; 360-569-2211.

Tom Barr

*Mount Rainier's peak looms behind Sunrise Visitor Center. The center, at 6,400 feet, is the highest point accessible by car.*

### North Cascades National Park

North Cascades' primeval landscape is sometimes referred to as "America's Alps." The park and Ross Lake and Lake Chelan National Recreation Areas encompass 674,000 acres of snow-capped peaks crisscrossed with networks of hanging glaciers, ice aprons, canyons, streams, and waterfalls. Most of the area is inaccessible by vehicle, and parts are too rugged for hikers. Some 318 glaciers lie within the park boundaries, offering superb mountaineering and backpacking opportunities.

National Park Service

*Much of North Cascades National Park remains a pristine wilderness*

The North Cascades Highway—Washington Highway 20—bisects the park and meanders through the Ross Lake Recreation Area. One of America's great scenic drives, it climbs to 4,860 feet at Rainy Pass and 5,477 feet at Washington Pass, and provides magnificent mountaintop views and fall colors, short hikes from the roadside, and viewable wildlife. Snow usually closes the highway from mid-November through April.

Much of the activity centers around the lakes, which offer fine fishing for several species of trout. Seattle City Light operates tours of Diablo Lake and Ross Dam hydro facilities. The *Lady of the Lake* cruises daily on 55-mile-long Lake Chelan to Stehekin. *FYI:* North Cascades National Park, 2105 Hwy. 20, Sedro Woolley; 360-856-5700.

Seattle City Light

*Seattle City Light has been operating tours on Diablo Lake for decades*

## Glacier Trivia

☞ Mount Rainier contains the largest and longest glaciers in the continental United States: 4.3-mile-long, 1-mile-wide Emmonds Glacier and 6-mile-long Carbon Glacier.

☞ Washington's Cascades contain approximately 756 glaciers, covering about 103 square miles.

☞ Approximately 80 percent of the glacier-covered areas in the contiguous U.S. are located in Washington.

☞ Approximately three-quarters of all the world's fresh water is stored in the earth's glaciers.

☞ An icefield is considered a glacier only when it begins to move.

## Mount St. Helens National Volcanic Monument

On May 18, 1980, Mount St. Helens erupted with a force equal to approximately 400 million tons of TNT. The eruption lasted nine hours, shortened the mountain by 1,300 feet, moved 4 billion cubic yards of earth, toppled 150 square miles of forest, and killed 57 people. Rocks, ash, and hot gas traveling up to 330 miles per

*For years after the 1980 eruption, Mount St. Helens was a barren landscape*

hour roared down the Toutle River Valley in history's largest landslide. The ash cloud rose to a height of 12 miles and circled the earth.

On the east side of the 110,000-acre National Monument, several Forest Service roads pass through sweeping views of blown-down forest en route to Windy Ridge, four miles from the crater and overlooking Spirit Lake. At the southern slope you can walk across lava flows, see lava casts of trees from a former eruption, and explore Ape Cave, Washington's longest lava tube.

Two west-side visitor centers feature interactive exhibits, a walk-in volcano, and a spectacular view of the only active volcano in the contiguous United States. Limited numbers of permits are issued during summer for summit climbs. During winter, some roads close. *FYI:* Headquarters, Amboy; 360-247-5473. Visitor Center, Castle Rock, five miles east of I-5 at Exit 49; 360-274-6644.

*The force of Mount St. Helens' eruption was equal to 400 million tons of TNT*

## Columbia River Gorge National Scenic Area

When Ice Age glaciers melted, more than 100 monstrous floods surged down the Columbia River, plowing this spectacular canyon through the Cascade Mountains.

As the only sea-level river flowing through the Cascades, the Columbia is both a natural wonder and an important transportation corridor. In this spectacular river canyon where high desert scrub brush meets lush forest, massive dams and river traffic are dwarfed in a landscape of meadows, valleys, towering cliffs, and rolling plateaus.

Washington Highway 14 hugs the river bank for 85 miles as it follows a mostly water-level route through the 235,500-acre Columbia River Gorge National Scenic Area. Across the river, the route is framed by Oregon's rugged cliffs topped by 11,245-foot, snow-capped Mt. Hood.

U.S. Forest Service

*Beacon Rock, on the Washington shore of the Columbia River Gorge, is the world's second-highest free-standing monolith*

The westward-flowing river and eastward-blowing wind have made the gorge a mecca for sailboarders. **Horsethief Lake** (509-767-1159) and **Maryhill State Parks** (509-773-5007) are popular riverside camping spots. At **Beacon Rock State Park** you can camp and climb the core of an 848-foot ancient volcano. *FYI:* 509-427-8265.

Columbia River stern-wheeler cruises depart from Stevenson, and hot springs have made Carson famous. The Klickitat and White Salmon Rivers are known for white water rafting, kayaking, canoeing, and fishing. Drano and Trout Lakes offer an alpine setting with good steelhead fishing. Meadows of mountain wildflowers reward springtime hikers.

Sightseeing attractions range from museums filled with coffee grinders, rosaries, and branding irons to the Bridge of the Gods, Bonneville Dam's turbines and fish ladders, and Goldendale Observatory's telescope. Maryhill Museum of Art and a full-sized Stonehenge replica are also located along the route. *FYI:* Columbia River Gorge National Scenic Area, 902 Wasco Avenue, Hood River, OR; 503-386-2333.

## The San Juan Islands

Of the 172 islands in the archipelago scattered over 179 square miles between Washington and Vancouver Island, British Columbia, about ten are inhabited. A popular way to sample the San Juans is by Washington State Ferry. Several ferries depart daily from Anacortes for Lopez, Shaw, Orcas, and San Juan Islands. *FYI:* Anacortes Visitor Information, 360-293-3832; Ferry schedules, 800-843-3779. The islands' slow pace and the protected waters, snug harbors, and idyllic countryside provide a sublime retreat from urban life.

Tom Barr

*Friday Harbor on San Juan Island is a departure point for whale-watching cruises, boating, and fishing*

San Juan Island, the most populous, attracts boaters, sea kayakers, saltwater fishermen, and whale watchers. The world's only museum devoted exclusively to whales, the nation's only whale-watching park, and the Pig War's San Juan Islands National Historic Park draw nature and history buffs. *FYI:* San Juan Island Visitor Information Service; 360-468-3663.

At 57 square miles, horseshoe-shaped Orcas is the largest island. Hilly and heavily forested, it includes **Moran State Park** with 5,000 acres of beaches, headlands, and freshwater lakes, four campgrounds, four waterfalls, and 30 miles of hiking trails. A narrow road spirals to the San Juans' highest point, 2,409-foot Mount Constitution, and exceptional views of the North Cascades and Olympic Mountains. *FYI:* 360-376-2326. Rosario, a turn-of-the-century mansion, forms the centerpiece of a popular resort with 180 modern rooms, a huge pipe organ, a museum, and several 1880s buildings. *FYI:* 360-376-2222 or 800-562-8820 in Washington.

Long and flat, Lopez is the perfect bicycler's island, with several beaches for strolling, picnicking, and camping. Franciscan nuns operate the ferry dock and general store at heavily forested Shaw, where overnight accommodations are limited to a county park with eight campsites.

Tom Barr

*Deception Pass, between the mainland and Whidbey Island, is one of Washington's most photographed sites*

## Whidbey Island

In 1985, Whidbey became the nation's largest island when the Supreme Court decided that New York's Long Island was really a peninsula. **Deception Pass State Park**'s beaches, campgrounds, freshwater lakes, and salt waters attract almost as many annual visitors as the Grand Canyon. *FYI:* Ten miles north of Oak Harbor; 360-675-2417.

The 45-mile-long by 3-to-10-mile-wide island is a patchwork of small farms and picturesque shoreline communities. Oak Harbor, the largest town, has a population of 18,930. Coupeville, called the Port of the Sea Captains, has been a popular retirement center for seafarers for over a century. In the 1880s a teenager became Langley's first settler when he bought 120 acres of land and sold wood to steamships. Today Langley, situated on a bluff overlooking the southern shoreline, is home to many painters, sculptors, potters, and jewelry makers. *FYI:* Central Whidbey Chamber of Commerce; 360-678-5434.

National Archives

*This 1888 Puget Sound crew is shipping a cargo of halibut*

## Puget Sound

Extending roughly from Everett to Olympia, Puget Sound touches Seattle, Tacoma, the Kitsap Peninsula, and the Olympic Peninsula's eastern edge. In the 1800s the fortunes of many Puget Sound communities were linked to processing seafood.

## The World's Longest . . .

Washington's Long Beach Peninsula, at 28 miles, and Dungeness Spit, at 5 miles, are the world's longest beach and sand spit. The Olympic Peninsula's 57 miles of undeveloped beach make it the world's longest wilderness shoreline.

## State Parks and Natural Areas

**The Channeled Scablands:** Lava flows and Ice Age floods that formed the Columbia Plateau and the Columbia River Gorge also created eastern Washington's Channeled Scablands. Near Odessa, volcanic explosions left numerous shallow basins ranging in diameter from a few hundred to 2,000 feet. Each crater has unique moats, dikes, circular walls, or other features. In spring many craters become temporary ponds surrounded by wildflowers. Driving, bicycling, and horseback trail maps are available from the Odessa Chamber of Commerce. *FYI:* 509-982-0188.

**Potholes Reservoir State Park:** Water remains year-round in many of the surrounding craters, forming more than 60 small lakes and ponds. The park's reservoir is a popular spot for trout fishing, sunbathing, and tent camping. *FYI:* 25 miles southwest of Moses Lake on Hwy. 170; 509-765-7271.

**Steptoe Butte State Park:** The tip of an ancient mountain protruding above more recent lava deposits offers an outstanding view of the checkerboard of fields below. *FYI:* 12 miles north of Colfax; 509-549-3551.

**Dry Falls:** During the Ice Age the Columbia River plunged over Dry

Falls in a volume equal to five Niagaras. When the river returned to its original channel, Dry Falls' cliff became a 400-foot-high, three-mile-wide skeleton. **Dry Falls Interpretive Center** (509-632-5214), perched on the chasm, exhibits bone chips from the Blue Lake Rhino, discovered near adjacent **Sun Lakes**

*Dry Falls is a remnant of the Ice Age*

State Park. The actual burial site is accessible via boat across the park's Blue Lake, or by hiking a rugged trail around the lake. *FYI:* Seven miles south of Coulee City, Hwy. 17; 509-632-5583.

**Ginkgo Petrified Forest State Park:** About 15 million years ago eastern Washington had a wet, tropical climate. It was the habitat of rhinoceroses, lions, camels, sabre-tooth tigers, and ginkgo trees, which now grow naturally only in China. At the visitor center you can see domestic ginkgo trees and Indian petroglyphs. A nature trail leads through ancient lake beds, lava flows, and petrified woods. *FYI:* One mile north of Vantage; 509-856-2700.

**The Palouse:** Spectacular canyons, cut through the fertile ash and loess by the Palouse and Snake Rivers, provide the base for some of the world's most productive wheat lands. *FYI:* Access to the canyons and rivers is offered at four state parks: **Chief Timothy**, 509-758-9580; **Lyons Ferry**, 509-646-3252; **Central Ferry** and **Palouse Falls**, 509-549-3551.

**Hell's Canyon:** Several Clarkston area tour operators offer scenic cruises on the Snake River into the rugged canyon that includes North America's deepest gorge.

**Fields Spring State Park:** A one-mile hike up 4,500-foot Puffer Butte provides sweeping views of Washington, Idaho, the Grande Ronde and Snake Rivers, and Oregon's Wallowa Mountains. *FYI:* 4.5 miles south of Anatone Hwy. 129; 509-256-3332.

Tom Barr

*Palouse Falls is one of southeastern Washington's most spectacular sites*

**Blue Mountains:** Formed some 200,000 years ago, the Blues offer rugged hiking and winter sports.

**Mima Mounds:** Geologists speculate that during glacial periods the ground cracked in a pattern of polygons. Ice formed in the crevices and then melted, leaving rounded cores. The mounds, about seven feet high and 70 feet wide, can be seen in fields along county roads south of Olympia near Little Rock.

## Million-Dollar Bulbs

In spring, when tulips, daffodils, and irises blossom, parts of western Washington turn every color of the rainbow. In the Skagit Valley, where flower bulbs are a $12-million-a-year business, thousands of people flock to see the fields in their full April splendor. A Puyallup farm grows more than 150 varieties of daffodils, crocuses, tulips, and hyacinths. Mossyrock in southwestern Washington is also a major commercial flower center.

## Big Rivers

Three major rivers flow through Washington. Along its 1,214 miles, the Columbia drains approximately 259,000 square miles of seven states and Canada. Like the Columbia, the Skagit River also flows out of British Columbia. It is fed by over 2,900 streams and more glaciers than any other river of the lower 48 states. The Snake River flows through Wyoming, Oregon, Idaho, and Washington, and is a key component of the Pacific Northwest transportation, fishery, and recreational resource network.

## Flora and Fauna

In Washington the plants and animals of the ocean and inland sea coexist with those of the desert and four mountain ranges.

Over 1,500 plants have been identified in the Cascade Mountains alone. The Olympic Mountains, Columbia River Gorge, Channeled Scablands, Hell's Canyon, and the Tumwater Botanical Area contain unique plants which grow nowhere else.

Seattle City Light

*Building Diablo and other dams on Washington's rivers was a massive undertaking, which sometimes involved literally moving mountains and towns*

Seals and sea lions share ocean waters with octopus, halibut, shad, smelt, herring, lingcod, rock fish, surf perch, Pacific cod, shrimp, and migrating gray whales. Orca whales inhabit the waters around the San Juan Islands. Oysters, crabs, and several species of clam share the shorelines. Salmon, bass,

*North Cascades mountain goat*

and trout swim rivers, streams, and lakes, and join sturgeon in the Columbia and Snake Rivers.

Birds migrate from as far as Mexico and Siberia. Roosevelt and Rocky Mountain elk, black and grizzly bears, mountain goats, bighorn sheep, deer, and cougar romp through the mountains. Western Washington has no poisonous snakes. But beware of the western rattlesnake in the Columbia Basin.

## Weathering the Weather

Washington's jumbled geology produces chaotic weather. Precipitation and temperatures vary greatly, depending on the location. Prime examples are Forks and Sequim, which are 70 miles apart but separated by the Olympic Mountains. Forks receives over 140 inches of rain per year while 17 inches falls at Sequim.

Seattle's annual rainfall is 36.2 inches — three less than Washington, D.C. and New York City. East of the Cascades, less than 20 inches of precipitation falls at Spokane, Yakima, and Walla Walla. Parts of western Washington experience below-freezing temperatures only 15 days per year, while eastern Washington snowfalls may stay for several months. Summertime highs average in the mid-70s to -80s in western Washington, and 90 degrees or above east of the mountains.

### Temperature Trivia

☞ Washington's record low temperature of −48 degrees Fahrenheit was recorded December 30, 1968, at Mazama and Winthrop. Ice Harbor Dam experienced the record high of 118 degrees Fahrenheit on August 5, 1961.

**Events**
**Forks Rain Festival:** Features umbrella-decorating and a carnival.
**Sequim Irrigation Festival:** Washington's oldest continuing festival celebrates the transformation of arid land into productive farms.
**Skagit Valley Tulip Festival:** The April festival features several weeks of flower field tours.

# CULTURES

## Native Americans

When the first explorers came to the Pacific Northwest there were more than 40 separate Indian tribes in Washington state.

The Cascade Mountains and the Indians' fear of thick, dense forests limited travel and ultimately divided them into two cultures, which anthropologists have termed the Coast or canoe Indians, and the Plateau or horse Indians. Both cultures shared some of the same beliefs and customs.

Washington tribes were not formal political organizations. Each village was an independent unit. Although several settlements might speak the same language, their relations were mostly social. The chief's major responsibilities were to settle quarrels, give feasts, and take care of the village's indigent.

Both cultures used magic to treat diseases. All tribes had secret societies, ceremonial dances and feasts, myths of creation, and beliefs about the hereafter. Both cultures believed that when time began, all things were living creatures, including earth, rocks, sky, and clouds. Thus every animate and inanimate object had a spirit. Since salmon yielded the greatest harvest, all tribes held salmon ceremonies. Securing the aid of a powerful guardian spirit who provided success in fishing, securing wealth, or other goals were also of prime importance.

Makah Museum

*Pacific Northwest tribes were expert craftspeople. This piece is carved in bone and shell.*

## Cultural Differences

Of all Native American societies, Coast Indians placed the most emphasis on accumulating private property, displaying wealth, and maintaining class differences. Slaves, taken in battle, were considered the lowest class and were commodities for trade or gifts. Next to the Southwestern pueblos, the coastal plank houses were Native Americans' most outstanding architectural feats. The homes generally accommodated six to 12 families, and feast houses sheltered several hundred people. Coast Indians also became adept at building dugout canoes—some were 50 feet long and 6 feet wide.

The horse and the need to travel farther to obtain food made the Plateau Indians more nomadic than their coastal counterparts. Wealth was measured mainly in the number of horses owned. There were few class distinctions. Slaves were treated as individuals and often became members of the captors' tribe. Leadership ability and wisdom were more important than wealth in selecting chiefs. Because Plateau Indians spent more time obtaining food, they had less time to devote to ceremonies and art.

While Washington Indians did not develop pottery, they became expert woodworkers, creating dishes, bowls, ladles, spoons, and wooden masks, representing animals or mythical creatures, for use in ceremonies. They also produced beautiful baskets and mats from tree and grass fibers.

© Makah Cultural and Research Center

*Makah Indian whaling and sealing canoes*

### Potlatches

Potlatches were unique to Pacific Northwest Coast Indians. Originally, a potlatch was an exhibition of an individual's wealth. At the elaborate feasts the host gave away most or all of his possessions. In preparation he stockpiled food to feed hundreds of guests for several weeks. Canoes, slaves, mats, blankets, jewelry, baskets, carved wooden boxes, and dishes were given to guests in order of their rank. When the potlatch ended the host would be temporarily destitute. Guests were expected to give the host presents which were more valuable than the ones they received.

## Tribal Warfare

Puget Sound villages were often enclosed in walled stockades, similar to traditional 1800s western forts. Tribal battles were fought to obtain slaves, or in retaliation. Often battles were brief and hostilities ceased after the first few casualties. Neither side expected total victory; both were satisfied with saving face. Some tribes treated battles like athletic events and alerted their enemies before coming to fight.

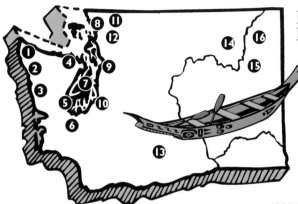

## Indian Reservations

While some Washington tribes were completely exterminated through disease and warfare, most were moved to the state's 26 Indian reservations. Several western Washington reservations were estab-

## Reservations

lished with the signing of the Point Elliott Treaty on January 22, 1855. The tribes received $150,000 in return for giving the United States roughly all the land between Tacoma and the Canadian border and from the Cascade Mountains to the Pacific Ocean. The total amounted to $1.80 a year over 20 years for each tribal member. It was paid, not in money, but in "useful articles." The treaty site is immortalized at **Mukilteo State Park** on Possession Sound. *FYI:* 206-353-2923.

### Western Washington Reservations

1) **Makah:** The westernmost reservation in the lower 48 states encompasses 24,526 acres. The Makahs have no linguistic association with any other U.S. tribe. Traditional basket weavings and wood carvings can be purchased at the Makah Cultural and Research Center, which displays 300- to 500-year-old artifacts. *FYI:* Makah Tribal Council, Neah Bay; 360-645-2201.

2) **Quileute:** The 800-acre reservation on an ocean harbor was established in 1855. It offers sport fishing and two popular resorts. *FYI:* Quileute Tribal Council, La Push; 360-374-6163.

3) **Quinault:** The largest Peninsula reservation extends from Lake

Quinault in Olympic National Park through the Quinault rain forest to the Pacific Ocean beaches. The tribe has jurisdiction over lake fishing. Roosevelt elk and wild rhododendrons are attractions on a 25-mile scenic-loop drive. Quinault Lodge, constructed in the 1920s, contains original furnishings and an extensive Northwest Indian art and basket collection. *FYI:* Quinault Indian Nation, Taholah; 360-276-8211.

**4) Jamestown Klallam:** With less than one square mile of land, this may be the nation's smallest Indian reservation. The Native Expressions Art Gallery in the tribal center features Northwest Coast native art. *FYI:* Jamestown Klallam Tribe, 305 Old Blyn Hwy., Sequim; 360-683-1109.

**5) Squaxin Island:** Under the 1854 Treaty of Medicine Creek, six tribes were consolidated on 2,000 acres rich in salmon, shellfish, and wildlife. Sa-heh-wa-mish, held in mid-June, features a pow-wow, art fair, and salmon bake. *FYI:* Squaxin Island Tribe, S.E. 70 Squaxin Lane, Shelton; 360-426-9781.

**6) Chehalis:** Established in 1864, the 2,600 acres were originally home to Chehalis, Chinook, Clatsop, and Cowlitz peoples. Camping, hunting, and fishing information is available through the tribal office. *FYI:* Chehalis Community Council, Oakville; 360-273-5911.

**7) Port Madison:** The two sections of the 8,012-acre reservation are situated on the Kitsap Peninsula. Totem poles, a famous agate beach, Chief Seattle's grave, the Suquamish Tribal Museum, and the beautiful setting make it a popular attraction. *FYI:* Suquamish Tribe, Suquamish; 360-598-3311.

**8) Lummi:** The 7,000-acre reservation overlooks the scenic San Juan Islands and includes a casino, a restaurant known for its salmon, and craft shops selling cedar bark baskets. *FYI:* Lummi Indian Nation, 2616 Kwina Road, Bellingham; 360-734-8180.

**9) Tulalip:** The 35,000-acre reservation, situated on scenic Tulalip Bay, offers a casino, bingo parlor, historic walking tour, totem poles, marina, and restaurant. *FYI:* Tulalip Tribes, 6700 Totem Beach Road, Marysville; 360-653-4585.

**10) Muckleshoot:** A casino, the state's second-oldest church, and gift shops featuring handcrafted native arts and Northwest Indian carvings are attractions on the 1,188-acre reservation in the western Cascade foothills. *FYI:* Muckleshoot Indian Tribe, 39015 172nd Ave, S.E., Auburn; 206-939-3311.

**11) Nooksack:** Reservation economy is based on commercial salmon, halibut, and shellfish harvesting. The tribal office issues permits for camping and fishing on Nooksack River tribal lands.

*FYI:* Nooksack Tribal Council, 5048 Mt. Baker Hwy., Deming; 360-592-5176.

**12) Upper Skagit:** Watching hundreds of bald eagles on the Skagit River, wilderness hiking, white water floats, skiing, and shell gathering are popular activities. *FYI:* Upper Skagit Indian Tribe, 2284 Community Plaza, Sedro-Woolley; 360-856-5501.

*Makah Indians on the beach at Port Townsend, en route to the hop fields of Puget Sound, ca. 1890*

National Archives

## Eastern Washington Reservations

**13) Yakima:** Washington's largest reservation spreads over 1.6 million acres of the Yakima Valley and eastern slopes of the Cascade Mountains. Yakima Indian Nation Cultural Center interprets the history with dioramas and exhibits. A gift shop sells Indian beadwork, and a restaurant serves Native American dishes. *FYI:* Confederated Tribes and Bands of the Yakima Indian Nation, Toppenish; 509-865-2800.

**14) Colville:** The 1.3 million acres are spread across northeastern Washington, Idaho, and eastern Oregon. Colville Museum and Gallery displays native art and traditional cedar baskets. Tribal-operated Lake Roosevelt marina rents houseboats. *FYI:* Colville Confederated Tribes, Nespelem; 509-634-4711.

**15) Spokane:** The 155,000-acre reservation, created in 1881, includes 44 miles of shoreline on Lake Roosevelt. A museum exhibits arrowheads, mortar, pestles, axe heads, and baskets. *FYI:* Spokane Tribe, Wellpinit; 509-258-4581.

Yakima Valley Museum

*Celilo Falls, now submerged by the backwaters of a dam, was a centuries-old Indian fishing spot*

**16) Kalispel:** Situated on the scenic Pend Oreille River, the 4,629-acre reservation offers boat launches, RV campgrounds, and fishing. *FYI:* Kalispel Tribe of Indians, Usk; 509-445-1147.

## Chief Sealth

Chief Sealth was born around 1786 on Bainbridge Island. A man of complex character and uncompromising integrity, he maintained a policy of non-resistance and cooperated with Seattle's first settlers, who named the town after him. "Seattle" was as close as they could come to pronouncing his name.

## Chief Joseph

Chief Joseph, leader of the Nez Perce, is buried at Nespelem on the Colville Reservation. He was known for his wisdom, eloquence, and humanitarianism. In October 1877 he led 400 men, women, and children in a running war with the U.S. Army through 12 engagements in a campaign that crossed the Bitter Root, Rocky, and Bear Paw Mountains.

Washington State University Special Collections

*Chief Joseph*

## Multiple Uses

Coastal Indians used virtually every part of the western red cedar. Logs were used for canoes and posts, split into planks, and carved into boxes, bowls, and ladles. The bark was twined into ropes and waterproof baskets, and shredded for baby diapers. It also made fringed skirts, rain capes, sails, and mats for bedding. The inner bark helped preserve berries for many months.

Tom Barr

*Passing parades of pleasure craft, container ships, and sightseeing vessels have made Ballard's locks one of the Seattle area's most visited spots*

## Ethnic Communities

Asians, Russians, Germans, Dutch, and Norwegians settled several communities in Washington. Today their heritages are displayed through their architecture, arts, crafts, and festivals.

**International District:** Seattle is the only Washington city to develop an organized Chinatown that attracts Asians from other areas of the state. Situated in south Seattle between the Kingdome and Interstate 5, this 40-square-block area is inhabited by Chinese, Japanese, Filipinos, and other Asians.

It began in the 1880s, when Chinese workers were imported to build railroads. During the 1886 depression, most were deported and replaced by Japanese, who took over their dwellings and jobs as laborers, launderers, and farmhands. In 1907 a Chinese investment group constructed hotels and shops, and the Japanese developed an adjacent community.

The multicultural heritage is reflected in numerous Chinese, Japanese, and Korean restaurants, herbalists, and acupuncturists. Colorful Chinese and Japanese signs decorate early 1900s storefronts. Upper-story outdoor balconies, characteristic of south China, are unique to the district. **Uwajimaya** is one of the Pacific Northwest's largest Japanese stores. *FYI:* 519 6th Ave. S.; 206-624-6248. The **Nippon Kan Theater**, a national historic site and a center of Japanese activities, presents a performing arts series. *FYI:* 628 S. Washington St.; 206-467-6807. Asian history and culture are interpreted at the **Wing Luke Asian Museum**. *FYI:* 407 7th Ave. S.; 206-623-5124.

Wing Luke Asian Museum

*Seattle has one of the largest Asian American communities in the U.S. This Japanese American family owned and operated Jim's Cafe in Seattle's Pioneer Square in the 1940s.*

**Ballard:** Now part of west Seattle, Ballard was settled by immigrants from Denmark, Finland, Norway, and Sweden. By 1895 it had the world's largest shingle industry. The circa 1890-1930 buildings of the Ballard Avenue Landmark District display Scandinavian flourishes. **Hiram M. Chittenden Locks**, also called Ballard Locks, serve over 100,000 boats annually as part of the eight-mile Washington Ship Canal linking lakes Union and Washington to Puget Sound. The site offers a 21-level fish ladder and a seven-acre ornamental garden. *FYI:* 3015 N.W. 54th St., 206-783-7001. Washington's Scandinavian culture is chronicled at the **Nordic Heritage Museum.** *FYI:* 206-789-5707. Ballard Chamber of Commerce, 2208 Market St.; 206-784-9705.

**Poulsbo:** This charming Kitsap Peninsula community exhibits its Norwegian heritage in several festivals, street names, outdoor murals, Viking statues, and statues of trolls on and in many of its shops. Situated on Liberty Bay, and bounded by Puget Sound's Hood Canal, it was settled in 1882 by fishermen, loggers, and farmers who found its surroundings similar to Norway's fjords. The town name means "Paul's Place," but bad handwriting and misinterpretation by the Postmaster General kept it Poulsbo. *FYI:* Greater Poulsbo Chamber of Commerce; 360-779-4848.

**Yakima Valley:** Hispanics comprise more than 30 percent of the valley's population and may account for 50 percent by the year 2000. Hispanic-owned companies are the valley's fastest growing businesses. The community of Granger has Washington's first non-profit Spanish-language radio station, which provides music, news, and public affairs programming. Cinco de Mayo, Fiestas Patrias, and a number of other Mexican festivals are held throughout the year in Wapato, Toppenish, Zillah, Sunnyside, Grandview, and Prosser. You'll also find an abundance of Mexican restaurants and a Taste of Mexico food fair at Grandview.

## More Ethnic Communities

**Lynden:** The first Dutch settlers arrived in 1900, attracted by the Nooksack Valley's rich farmland and its resemblance to the Netherlands. Today more than half of the community's 6,480 residents are of Dutch descent. The heritage

*Lynden and Oak Harbor celebrate their Dutch heritage with annual festivals*

Lynden Chamber of Commerce

lives on in restaurants, an inn with a four-story windmill, and a shopping mall that flies provincial flags of the homeland. Lynden also has an interior Holland street market with a canal and Dutch-style bridges. *FYI:* Chamber of Commerce, 444 Front St., Delft Square; 360-354-5995.

**Oak Harbor:** Several nationalities helped settle Whidbey Island's largest community. The first claims were staked in the 1850s by a Norwegian shoemaker, a New Englander, and a Swiss army officer. They were followed by Irish farmers and fishermen and later, Hollanders. A windmill overlooking the scenic harbor, Holland Gardens, and annual ethnic events celebrate the various influences. *FYI:* Greater Oak Harbor Chamber of Commerce; 360-675-3535.

**Bingen/White Salmon:** The towns were settled in the 1850s. Their railroad depot earned them mention in *Ripley's Believe It or Not* as the nation's only depot with the names of two towns. Named for "Bingen-on-the-Rhine" by a German settler, Bingen lies on flat land, while White Salmon perches on the bluffs above. Columbia River sailboarding has diversified the towns' wood products-based economy. *FYI:* Mt. Adams Chamber of Commerce; 509-493-3630.

**Odessa:** In the late 1700s Catherine the Great promised Germans automony if they would come to Russia to colonize the Volga. After she died, the promise was broken. Between 1900 and 1910, to escape oppression, many of their descendants emigrated to Washington and became wheat farmers in Odessa. Great Northern Railroad officials named the town after the Russian seaport. Approximately 80 percent of the population is of German/Russian descent. Some early red-brick buildings exhibit a combination of Victorian, Volga, and Black Sea architecture. Two sausage factories make foods with centuries-old recipes brought from the Volga colonies. *FYI:* Odessa Chamber of Commerce; 509-982-0188.

**Leavenworth:** It looks like an authentic Bavarian village, so it must be one. Right? Not really. Platted in 1892, Leavenworth became one of the first communities in Washington to use irrigation, and established itself as a fruit production center. In 1963 someone decided that with gabled roofs,

*Leavenworth turned itself into an award-winning Bavarian village that is a must-see for everyone*

timbered exteriors, painted stucco buildings, and other accoutrements, it would be everyone's idea of a typical Bavarian mountain village. Several festivals, complete with Bavarian costumes, foods, dancers, and *oompa* bands, turned the theme into reality and have made the town one of Washington's top visitor attractions. Perched near the summit of the Cascades and surrounded by towering mountain peaks, it is also a popular winter sports area. *FYI:* Leavenworth Chamber of Commerce; 509-548-5807.

*Delightful figurines and paintings decorate Leavenworth's shops*

## Native American Events

**Tinowit Annual International Powwow:** Native dancers from tribes throughout the United States gather at Yakima in July.

**Chief Seattle Days:** The August event at Suquamish celebrates Chief Seattle, hereditary leader of the Suquamish Indians, with a salmon bake, canoe races, powwow, and dancing.

**Spokane Indian Days:** War dances, games, and other events continue 24 hours a day over Labor Day weekend at the Spokane Indian Reservation.

**Yakima Nation Indian Days Celebration:** The multi-day September event at White Swan features war dancing and drumming contests, stick games, and arts and crafts.

**Wenatchee River Salmon Festival:**
Each October the return of
the salmon is celebrated near
Leavenworth with a Native
American fishing village, interpretive trail, children's activities,
and an outdoor aquarium.

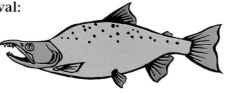

*Colorful Scandinavian costumes decorate a Ballard bus shelter and are often seen in ethnic festivals*

Tom Barr

## Ethnic Festivals

**Great Bavarian Ice Fest:** Snow sculpting, dogsled races, weight-pulling contests, sleigh rides, cross-country ski races, a smooching contest, and ice cube hunt for kids are featured in Leavenworth in January.

**Festival Sundiata:** The Pacific Northwest's largest celebration of African American culture, history, and art is free and takes place in Seattle during February.

**Hoquiam Ethnic Heritage Festival:** A variety of ethnic groups are represented at local events, dinners, booths, and shows in March.

**Finnish-American Folk Festival:** Naselle, near the mouth of the Columbia River, features crafts, demonstrations, food, and children's activities in April.

**Holland Happening:** An April-May celebration of Dutch heritage with arts and crafts fair, international dancing, and food booths at Oak Harbor.

**Holland Days Festival:** Reenactments of Dutch customs, Dutch games, wooden shoe race, *klompen* dancing at Lynden in May.

**Leavenworth Maifest:** Features Bavarian dancers, *oompa* bands, street dancing, food.

**White Salmon Maifest:** Offers Bavarian crafts, food, dancing.

**Skandia Midsommarfest:** Scandinavian pole raising, Nordic music and folk dancing, traditional crafts, and ethnic foods at Poulsbo in June.

**Scottish Highland Games:** Piping, drumming, highland dancing, stock dog trials, and clan craft tents are part of the June event at Ferndale.

**Chinatown International District Summer Festival:** This July event showcases the essence of the community with costumed dancers, over 70 food and arts and crafts booths, children's activities, and karate and other demonstrations.

**Odessa Deutschesfest:** The September event offers locally made *kraut ranzas*, apple strudel and other German/Russian foods, German music, and a block-long *Biergarten*.

Lynden Chamber of Commerce

*Lynden's Holland Days Festival features parades, wooden shoe races, and* klompen *dancers*

**Octoberfest:** The late September–early October event in Stevenson includes a Norwegian draft horse show, Columbia River Gorge wines, local beer, and German specialty foods.

**Washington State Autumn Leaf Festival:** Live music and authentic Bavarian foods highlight the September event in Leavenworth.

**St. Demetrios Greek Festival:** Greek food, pastries, dancing, art, icon paintings, and church tours are part of the October event in Seattle.

**Italian Heritage Days:** Walla Walla's October event includes Italian cuisine, a Columbus Parade, Tarantella folk dancing, and a grape stomp.

**Ballard Nordic Yulefest:** Pre-Christmas holiday fair with music, Norwegian dancing, crafts, children's activities, and Scandinavian food and drink.

**Yule Fest:** During December, modern-day Vikings arrive by boat at Poulsbo, escorting Lucia Bride to shore for yule log lighting and torchlight parade. Scandinavian foods, crafts, Sons of Norway bazaar.

**Leavenworth Lighting Festival:** Bandstand music, snowman contest, sleigh rides, Bavarian foods, evening concerts, simultaneous lighting of the village in December.

# GOING TO TOWN

Tom Barr

*Olympia has been Washington's capital since territorial days*

## Olympia

**Pop.** 36,520
**Elev.** 36 feet
**Noted for:** State Capitol, State Capitol Museum, Washington State Capitol Historic District, Yashiro Japanese Garden, scenic waterfront promenade.
**Nearby:** Wolf Haven, Mima Mounds, Hood Canal, Fort Lewis, Nisqually National Wildlife Refuge, Millersylvania State Park.
**Visitor's Information:** 360-586-3460

Olympia is an important seaport and manufacturing center. A sawmill was built there in 1848, signaling the dawn of Puget Sound's commercial era. Olympia's location and water access led to its designation as the territorial capital in 1853. Several challenges to move the capital failed, and it has remained the seat of state government ever since.

When the biennial legislature is in session, Olympia bustles with activity. Otherwise it has a casual, relaxed ambiance. The stately Romanesque legislative building with a 287-foot dome perches on a bluff overlooking Budd Inlet. A large, open, grass-covered courtyard with rose gardens and Japanese cherry trees surrounds the Capitol Campus. Visitors can tour the Executive Mansion and watch sessions from the visitor's gallery.

Olympia has been chosen by several national magazines as one of the most livable cities in the nation. Many downtown buildings and early 20th century homes are listed on the National Register. Funds and labor donated by Olympia's sister city, Yashiro, Japan, helped build the Japanese Garden, which features a waterfall, bamboo grove, carp pond, and stone lanterns.

### Olympia Events
May–Wooden Boat Festival
July–Capitol City Marathon and Lakefair
Labor Day Weekend–Vintage Tugboat Race

# Seattle

**Pop.** 527,700
**Elev.** 0-512 feet
**Noted for:** Pike Place Market, Space Needle, Seattle Center, Ballard Locks, Museum of Flight, Woodland Park Zoo, Seahawks NFL football, Mariners Major League baseball, Supersonic NBA basketball, waterfront, Pioneer Square, International District, Seattle Art Museum, Klondike Gold Rush National Historic Park.
**Nearby:** Tillicum Indian Village, Snoqualmie Falls, Dash Point State Park, Saltwater State Park.
**Visitor's Information:** 206-461-5800

Seattle's first settlers filed claims in 1851 when they realized that Elliott Bay would provide easy access for shipping. The city's early economy was based on timber, coal mining, and railroads. It recovered from a devastating 1889 fire, which consumed 50 blocks, by becoming the major debarkation point for the Klondike Gold Rush of 1897.

Seattle is still surrounded by evergreen forest and salt- and fresh-water shoreline. It is the commercial, cultural, financial, and advanced technology hub of the Pacific Northwest and a major port city for trans-Pacific and European trade. In addition to aerospace and computer software and equipment, major industries include outdoor recreation equipment, sportswear, food products, wood products, fish processing, medical equipment, biotechnology, environmental engineering, and electronic and measurement instruments. The Port of Seattle is the top U.S. port in container tonnage exports to Asia, and one of the largest containers ports in the world.

Tom Barr

*Condominiums, restaurants, and parks surround Lake Union, a favorite of boaters*

Seattle Center, a 74-acre urban park, is the city's entertainment and cultural heart, and Pike Place Market is its soul.

## Seattle Festivals
May–Northwest Folklife
July–Bite of Seattle
July-August–Seafair
Labor Day Weekend–Bumbershoot

Tom Barr

*Old City Hall is one of many historic buildings preserved in Tacoma*

# Tacoma

**Pop.** 181,200
**Elev.** 87 feet
**Noted for:** Tacoma Dome; Point Defiance Park; Tacoma Art Museum; Washington State Historical Society Museum; W.W. Seymour Botanical Conservatory; Old Town Historic District.
**Nearby:** Mount Rainier National Park and scenic railroad; Kitsap and Olympic Peninsulas; Gig Harbor; Northwest Trek; Dash Point State Park; Saltwater State Park; Enchanted Village Amusement Park; Lakewood Gardens; Fort Lewis Military Museum; McChord Air Museum.
**Visitor's Information:** 206-627-2836

Once called the City of Destiny, Tacoma has become an important industrial center and major seaport, and vies with Spokane for the title of Washington's second largest city. An early developer with a history of promoting non-existent towns and selling land sight unseen to gullible investors saw Tacoma's possibilities as a railroad terminus. The Northern Pacific Railway arrived in 1873, turning the city into an important coaling station. Wood products, fishing, shipping, and copper smelting diversified the economy, but earned it a bad reputation for pollution.

A 1980s revitalization program cleaned up the air, spread the economic base, refurbished historic buildings, and developed various artistic endeavors and attractions. The Tacoma Dome, the world's largest wood dome arena, hosts conventions, trade shows, and major musical events. With the world's fifth largest deep-water harbor, Tacoma attracts electronics manufacturers, seafood processors, foreign-owned corporations, and automobile importers. The historic district offers a melange of antique and collectible shops, boutiques, and small restaurants.

## Tacoma Events
April–Daffodil Festival
September–Port of Tacoma Annual Free Boat Tours
December–First Night Pierce County

**Port Angeles:** In 1954 the Olympic Peninsula's largest town and county seat was the first Northwest community honored as an "All-American City." Captain Francisco Eliza named the harbor "Porto de Nuestra Senora de Los Angeles" or Port of Our Lady of the Angels, in

*Port Angeles is the gateway to Olympic National Park*

Olympic National Park

1791. In 1862 President Abraham Lincoln set aside 3,520 acres for a lighthouse and military reservation. After the lighthouse was built, the remaining land was opened for townsites. Port Angeles was the only city built under this provision, and it became known as America's second national city (Washington, D.C., being the first).

The Port of Port Angeles operates two deep-water mine terminals, and the city's Boat Haven is home to over 563 pleasure craft. Scuba diving, crabbing, clam digging, beach combing, and fresh- and salt-water fishing are popular pursuits. **Noted for:** gateway to the Olympic Peninsula and Victoria, British Columbia. *FYI:* Chamber of Commerce; 360-452-2363.

**Port Townsend:** In the late 1800s rumors of railroads, which never materialized, sparked two Victorian building booms. Rowdy waterfront taverns and bordellos led city fathers to proclaim "Sin flourishes at sea level," and a genteel business district was built uptown. Some 70 buildings from the waterfront and several streets of

Port Townsend Chamber of Commerce

*Port Townsend's Victorian seaport*

Victorian homes are preserved as a National Historic Landmark. Port Townsend is considered the best example of a Victorian seaport town north of San Francisco. A full slate of festivals, dinner theaters, and concerts keeps the economy alive and visitors coming back for more. **Noted for:** Victorian homes, performing arts festivals, Fort Worden State Park. *FYI:* Chamber of Commerce; 360-385-2722.

# Bellingham

**Pop.** 55,480
**Elev.** 68 feet
**Noted for:** Port of Entry; Fairhaven Historical District; Western Washington University outdoor sculpture collection; Mount Baker Theater; Whatcom Museum of History and Art; May Ski to Sea Festival.
**Nearby:** Chuckanut Drive; Birch Bay State Park; San Juan Islands; Peace Arch State Park; Semiahmoo Resort; Lake Terrell Wildlife Preserve; Point Roberts; Lynden; Lake Whatcom; Mount Baker Scenic Byway; Larrabee State Park.
**Visitor's Information:** 800-487-2032

*Bellingham is the southern terminus for the Alaska State Ferry System*

Bellingham Convention and Visitors Bureau

Captain George Vancouver named the bay after the British Admiralty's Sir William Bellingham. An 1852 coal discovery brought settlement, and six years later the Fraser River Gold Rush generated a tent city supply center. It folded quickly when the British Columbia government insisted miners report to Victoria prior to leaving for the diggings. With the establishment of a sawmill and railroad, fishing, canning, and farming followed.

Bellingham's waterfront supports fishing, boat building, shipping, paper processing, and marina operations. The town is a consolidation of four communities, which exhibit an array of vintage homes built between 1880 and 1910.

# Point Roberts

This Washington community is a "geographic and political accident" created in 1846 when the 49th parallel was established as the boundary between Canada and the U.S. It is not connected to the United States. From Washington, by land it is accessible only by crossing into Canada at Blaine, traveling west to Tsawwassen, heading south, and crossing the border again. Its attractions include **Lighthouse Marine Park**, whale watching, and clam digging.
*FYI:* 811 Marine Dr., 360-945-4911; Chamber of Commerce, 360-945-2313.

# Vancouver

**Pop.** 55,450
**Elev.** 42 feet
**Noted for:** Fort Vancouver National Historic Site; Pearson Airpark; Officers' Row Victorian buildings; Columbia River Gorge.
**Nearby:** Portland, Oregon; Mount St. Helens National Volcanic Monument; Battleground Lake State Park; Lewis River Excursion Train; Cedar Creek Grist Mill; Ridgefield National Wildlife Refuge; Hulda Klager Lilac Gardens.
**Visitor's Information:** 360-693-1313

Named in honor of Captain George Vancouver, Washington's oldest community grew up around the Hudson's Bay Company fur trading post established in 1825. After the United States took possession in 1846, it garrisoned Fort Vancouver, and the city was incorporated in 1857. Among the officers who served at the fort were Ulysses S. Grant, Phillip Sheridan, Benjamin Bonneville, George C. Marshall, and Omar Bradley.

*Gaches Mansion is one of many fine Victorian homes along Vancouver's Officers' Row*

Tom Barr

Steamboats, gold discoveries, and the completion of the Northern Pacific Railroad to Tacoma stimulated growth. During the 1890s Vancouver produced so many prunes that a local military company recruited for the Spanish-American War was known as the "Prune Picked Platoon." Pearson Airpark dates to a 1905 dirigible landing and is the nation's oldest operating airfield. A Soviet transpolar monument honors three Moscow aviators who made the world's first non-stop transpolar flight and landed here June 20, 1937.

Today's diversified economy includes manufacturing, microelectronics, and technical engineering companies.

## Vancouver Events
May–Fort Vancouver Queen Victoria Birthday Celebration
June–Where Summer Begins Festival
June–Fort Vancouver Days
July–Fort Vancouver Brigade Encampment
August–Northwest Antique Airplane Club Fly-In

## Searching for Utopia

Washington's first utopian community, the Puget Sound Cooperative Colony, was started in 1877 at Port Angeles. The colony, which held its land in common trust, dissolved a few years later when members began charging each other with fraud. In 1897 three families founded the Mutual Home Colony Association, a utopian community of peace-loving anarchists, near Tacoma. After a free-love policy and arrests for nude bathing brought unwanted notoriety, its 200 members gradually abandoned their doctrines.

### Town Trivia

☞ The term "skid row" originated in Seattle in 1853, when logs were dragged by teams of oxen over a muddy road to the mill. Because of its slick surface, it was called the skid road. Soon it was lined with saloons and brothels, and the phrase became a euphemism for sleaze and degradation.

☞ Seattle is said to be the best U.S. city in which to have a heart attack because over half the adult population has some CPR training.

☞ Kelso is known as the Smelt Capital of the World.

### Community Quiz

1) George Washington, the biracial son of an ex-slave, founded _____ in 1875.
   **a)** Yelm          **b)** Centralia     **c)** Roslyn

2) Smuggler "Dirty Dan" Harris jumped ship in Vancouver and founded _____.
   **a)** Friday Harbor     **b)** Anacortes     **c)** Fairhaven

3) Harry Tracy, one of the Old West's last outlaws, died in a wheatfield near _____.
   **a)** Starbuck          **b)** Creston     **c)** Pullman

# Spokane

**Pop.** 183,800
**Elev.** 1,898-2,356 feet
**Noted for:** Riverfront Park; Fairchild Air Force Base; Gonzaga University; Walk in the Wild Zoo; Finch Arboretum; Cheney Cowles Museum; Lilac Festival (May).
**Nearby:** 76 freshwater lakes within a 50-mile radius; Turnbull National Wildlife Refuge; Mount Spokane State Park; Idaho's Coeur d'Alene Lake and Resort.
**Visitor's Information:** 509-624-1341; out of state, 800-248-3230.

Although the North West Company established a trading post here in 1810, the area remained unsettled until 1872. After two Montana cattlemen staked claims near Spokane Falls, the inevitable sawmill followed, and the Northern Pacific Railway made it a transportation center. Spokane sputtered along until 1889, when fire destroyed the entire business district; then it zoomed to 19,000 people during the next year.

During the 1990s Spokane has challenged Tacoma as Washington's second biggest city. The largest city between Seattle, Calgary, Minneapolis, and Salt Lake City, Spokane serves parts of four states, British Columbia, and Alberta. Shoppers navigate through downtown on a weatherproof skywalk system connecting a 15-block area.

Riverfront Park straddles the Spokane River. It offers amusement rides, mini-golf, an ice rink, and Imax Theater. The city's name comes from a local Indian tribe and means "children of the sun."

## Speaking in Spokane

In 1909 members of the Industrial Workers of the World (Wobblies) spoke in Spokane and were arrested. When they argued that officials were interfering with their right of free speech, newspapers printed the story and it became a national event. Over 1,000 people were arrested before the ordinance banning the demonstrations was removed.

## Tri-Cities
**Pop.** 105,070
**Elev.** 360 feet
**Noted for:** Wine Country; Hanford Science Center; Sacajawea State Park; Columbia Cup Unlimited Hydroplane Race.
**Nearby:** Columbia River Gorge; Snake and Yakima Rivers; Horse Heaven Hills; Benton County Historical Museum; McNary National Wildlife Refuge; Ice Harbor Dam.
**Visitor's Information:** 509-735-8486 or 800-666-1929

Tom Barr

*Pasco County Courthouse is the seat of Franklin County government*

Kennewick, Pasco, and Richland comprise the Tri-Cities metropolitan area. While the area receives only seven inches of rain per year, the Columbia, Snake, and Yakima Rivers converge here, providing ample irrigation for row crops, livestock, wheat, apples, peaches, cherries, potatoes, alfalfa, mint, and corn. Over 25 wineries are located within a 50-mile radius, and the cities are transportation hubs for the Columbia Basin, Palouse wheat country, and Yakima Valley.

Transportation and irrigation played major roles in the region's development. Pasco was founded in 1880 by Northern Pacific Railroad construction crews, who named it Pasco because the intense heat, winds, and storms reminded them of Peru's Cerro de Pasco. The first heavier-than-air airport west of the Mississippi was built at Pasco in 1910, and the first U.S. airmail service started here in 1926.

Construction of locks and dams on the Columbia in the 1930s transformed the Tri-Cities into major energy and river transportation centers. When Hanford Atomic Works was built during World War II, Richland's population exploded from 300 to over 15,000 in one year.

**Tri-Cities Events**
June–Tri-Cities Wineries Barrel Tasting
July–Budweiser Columbia Cup Hydroplane Race
September–Catch the Crush Wine Festival
November–Tri-Cities Northwest Wine Festival

# Yakima

**Pop.** 59,580
**Elev.** 1,068 feet
**Noted for:** 23 wineries; fruit production; Yakima River Canyon; Tieton River white water; Yakima Valley Community College; North Front Street Historical District; Yakima Valley Museum and Historical Association horse-drawn vehicle collection.
**Nearby:** Toppenish murals; Fort Simcoe State Park; Yakima Nation Cultural Center; White Pass ski area; Oak Creek Wildlife Area; Central Washington Agricultural Museum; Mount Rainier National Park; William O. Douglas Wilderness; Ellensburg Historic District; Olmstead Place Pioneer Farm.
**Visitor's Information:** 509-575-1300 or 800-221-0751

*By 1918 Yakima was a bustling trade center serving a large area of central Washington*

Yakima Valley Museum

This county seat was once a hunting, fishing, and meeting place for Yakima Indian tribes. When the railroad came in 1883, it attempted to buy Yakima City land for rail yards, but some residents refused to sell. The Northern Pacific platted a new town four miles north. After it offered to move Yakima City's buildings, over 50 homes, stores, saloons, hotels, and the courthouse were dragged by horse and oxen teams to the new community. Businesses remained open and operated during the transfer. Yakima City was renamed Union Gap.

In the early 1900s irrigation systems transformed dry land into farms and established the valley as one of the world's most diversified agricultural regions. It leads the nation in the number of fruit trees and production of apples, mint, winter pears, and hops, and is fourth in the value of combined fruit grown.

## Yakima Events
April–Spring Barrel Tasting
May–Cherry Blossom Festival
May–Yakima Air Fair
November–Thanksgiving in the Wine Country

**Walla Walla:** The retail, medical, and professional center of southeastern Washington and northeastern Oregon was making history long before the town was established. Whitman Mission was a supply center and stopover point for Oregon Trail immigrants. Fort Walla Walla was built in 1858, and the town grew up around it. Gold discoveries turned it into a rowdy boom town with outlaws, rustlers, and justice by vigilante committees. Whitman College, a four-year liberal arts school, is the oldest college in Washington State. **Noted for:** wheat, green peas, onions, Whitman Mission National Historic Site, Balloon Stampede, historic homes. *FYI:* Chamber of Commerce; 509-525-0850.

**Wenatchee:** According to local Indian lore, Wenatchee means "robe of the rainbow." Although Wenatchee was crossed by fur traders, missionaries, prospectors, miners, supply trains, and railroads, it took construction of the 25-mile-long Highline Canal in 1903 to make the area boom. In the self-proclaimed "Apple Capital of the World," the 180-day growing season and summer temperatures in the 90s and 100s also produce bumper crops of cherries, pears, and peaches. **Noted for:** Washington State University Tree Fruit Research Center, Washington State Apple Commission, river rafting, sailboarding, snow skiing. *FYI:* 800-57-APPLE.

---

**Tokyo-Wenatchee Nonstop**

On October 5, 1931, the first nonstop flight across the Pacific Ocean ended at East Wenatchee's Fancher Field. It originated in Tokyo and took 41 hours and 13 minutes. The aircraft carried tins of survival food, extra fuel tanks, a reinforced undercarriage, and wheels which could be jettisoned in flight. When one of the wheels stuck, pilot Clyde Pangborn climbed out in mid-flight and released it over Alaska's Aleutian Islands, thus necessitating a belly landing in Wenatchee. The Pangborn-Herndon Memorial at Fancher Field honors Pangborn and co-pilot Hugh Herndon Jr.

## Twin Towns

Many small towns in Washington are situated in pairs, separated by less than five miles.

**Clarkston, Washington and Lewiston, Idaho:** Although several hundred miles from the ocean, the towns are major ports and the gateway to Hell's Canyon.

**Okanogan and Omak:** The city limits of the two come within 100 yards of each other. Okanogan is the seat of government for Washington's largest county, and Omak is its commercial center. They are the home of one of Washington's outstanding small museums and the Omak Stampede and Suicide Race.

**Ocean Shores and Westport:** Ocean Shores is a resort and conference center. Whale-watching and fishing charters have brought Westport fame.

**Ilwaco and Long Beach:** Ilwaco's economy is based in charter fishing. Long Beach is a popular summer resort, winter retreat, and Washington's kite-flying mecca.

**Aberdeen and Hoquiam:** Kurt Cobain and Nirvana started in Aberdeen. Hoquiam's fame rests on superb wildlife watching, murals, Hoquiam's Castle, and other fine Victorian-era buildings.

**Centralia and Chehalis:** Centralia exhibits a mixture of Victorian homes and 1920s commercial buildings, and an outdoor mural gallery. Chehalis is the Lewis County seat.

**Kelso and Longview:** In 1923 the Long-Bell Lumber Company built the world's largest sawmill across from Kelso along with one of the first planned communities. The Cowlitz County Museum is located in Kelso.

# TASTE OF WASHINGTON

Tom Barr

*Pike Place Market, the soul of Seattle, is the oldest continuously operated farmer's market in the nation*

## Fresh! Local Ingredients! Seasonal!

These are the the hallmarks of the emerging Northwest cuisine. While many agree there is no established Northwest cuisine, there is an evolving philosophy and style.

The philosophy is not tied to tradition. At its heart is the use of fresh local ingredients cooked with sauces, herbs, and spices that enhance natural flavors while providing nutritious composition that lowers fat and protein and increases carbohydrates. That thinking, according to some, is a true Northwest phenomenon.

### How Fresh Is Fresh?

Raw materials must be of the highest quality and cooked when taste and aroma are at their best. Some Washingtonians wouldn't think of eating imported winter strawberries when they could wait a few months and pick them fresh. Corn off the stalk for a few hours is a waste of time, and seafood a few days old isn't very good either.

Although the ideal in cooking is to do as little to the food as possible, it is a very complex, subtle cuisine. Washington's cyclical seasons shape the food gathering and make it possible to eat supremely well.

## Nature's Cornucopia

For some the season begins in January, when oily smelt leave the ocean and swim up rivers. For others, it's the appearance of hothouse rhubarb in February. Many hold out for April's asparagus, then make a pilgrimage to the Yakima Valley and pick it wild along roadsides and streams, or wait a bit longer and buy it fresh from markets or roadside stands. In April hikers beat the Cascades bushes for mushrooms. There they may find over 50 edible species, 20 of which are considered choice.

Coinciding with the April-June asparagus-rhubarb season come sweet peas, Pacific shrimp, and an assortment of freshwater fish. Overlapping them are winter cauliflower and broccoli, followed by spinach, lettuce, pod peas, and green beans. In late May and early June the horn of plenty opens up with cabbages, squash, summer cauliflower, broccoli, corn, tomatoes, Walla Walla sweet onions, spring lamb, and sea-run salmon. Chinook salmon are followed by sockeye, pink, coho, and chum salmon, as well as sturgeon and shad.

## The Nation's Fruit Bowl

Washington enjoys a natural bounty of wild and commercially-grown fruits and vegetables. Late May and early June bring strawberries. The ripening continues through summer in a progression of raspberries, salmonberries, timbleberries, wild dewberries, domestic blueberries, Himalayan blackberries, wild huckleberries, mountain blueberries, and wild and domestic cranberries. In mid-June and July come cherries, apricots, peaches, plums, and the first apples. A variety of apples ripen through fall along with pears and wine grapes. The autumn larder can also be supplemented with wild duck, geese, deer, and elk.

*Local produce is a long-established industry in Washington*

Winter is the best time for catching crabs and steelhead trout, and for eating oysters.

## Ethnic Diversity

Although Northwest cuisine has been emerging for only 15 to 20 years, local cooking has absorbed a vast array of influences, including a couple of centuries of Indian, European, and other cuisines. International trade has brought the aromas of Mexico, Japan, China, and other countries. Along with American basics such as barbecue and fried chicken, you'll also find Italian, Ethiopian, Swedish, Mediterranean, Greek, French, Thai, Caribbean, Moroccan, African, Israeli, Iraqi, Cajun, Creole, and Lebanese food.

Tom Barr

*Crabs shed their shells. They are best when shells are hard.*

## Seeking Safe Seafood

Washington seafood is internationally famous for its abundance and variety, including mussels, oysters, five species of clams, several crabs, five types of fresh- and salt-water salmon, plus an assortment of trout, bass, and bottom fish.

When selecting frozen fish, make sure it has been bled, gutted, and iced to 32 degrees on board the fishing vessel. Fresh fish do not smell fishy. The skin should retain at least 80 percent of its scales. Fish fillets should have a translucent, glistening look.

To ensure freshness, shellfish should be purchased live. Do not cook or eat shellfish if shells are open or broken. Throw them away if you can open them with your fingers, or if they do not open during cooking.

### Sexually Confused Oysters

Oysters are at their most succulent during the winter months. When the water heats up, so do oysters' sexual urges, and they become soft, milky, and thin. Researchers have developed a method of sexually confusing oysters so they remain plump, crisp, and tasty during the warm months.

Yakima Valley Visitors and Convention Bureau

*Washington leads the nation in growing hops, natural preservatives that enhance the foam and quality of beer*

## Cash Crops

Washington leads the nation in growing 12 commodities and ranks in the top ten for an additional 19 crops. It is first in apples, Concord grapes, sweet cherries, pears, processed carrots, asparagus, red raspberries, hops, lentils, dry peas, Italian prune plums, and spearmint oil. Over 90 percent of the nation's supply of hothouse rhubarb and over 50 percent of fresh field rhubarb come from Washington. Washington grows more wheat per acre than any other dryland farming area.

*Washington has led the nation in apple production every year except one since the 1920s*

## Apples

Washington's apple industry dates back to 1889. Over 50 percent of the nation's apples are grown here and shipped to more than 30 nations. If the entire annual apple crop were laid side by side, it would stretch from Seattle to New York City and back 65 times.

## Walla Walla Sweets

Along with salmon, apples, and asparagus, Washingtonians share at least one other passion—the Walla Walla Sweet Onion. It was developed through years of experimentation and cross-breeding to produce an onion that could be planted in fall, survive winter snows, and mature in spring. Sometime after 1900 the Walla Walla Sweet attained cult status, acquiring an official historian, a registered logo, and a trademark. The logo, featuring an onion in front of a blue mountain, is the only way to be sure you're getting the genuine article. As anyone who's ever eaten a Walla Walla Sweet will tell you, the best way to enjoy them is to eat them raw. Their mild taste distinguishes them from other yellow onions. Many people eat them like apples. They're also guaranteed not to make your eyes water when you cut and peel them.

*Washington apple orchards range from 35 to 3,000 acres, and a typical tree yields 600 to 700 pounds of fruit*

## Taste-Tempting Recipes

The following recipes incorporate wild or domestic ingredients commonly found or grown in Washington State.

### Berry Berry

Washington is one of the nation's few significant cranberry-growing states. Three major areas on the Washington coast near Hoquiam,

*While food fairs in the early 1900s emphasized seasonings, today's festivals, such as the Bite of Seattle and various seafood events, are likely to emphasize the natural ingredients of the foods*

Everett Public Library

Grayland, and the Long Beach Peninsula produce an annual crop of about 12 million pounds. The **Pacific Coast Cranberry Museum** details the industry's history with tools, labels, sorters, and other unique equipment. *FYI:* Pioneer Road, Long Beach; 360-642-4938.

### Cranberry Bread

2 cups all-purpose flour
1 cup sugar
1½ teaspoons double acting baking powder
½ teaspoon baking soda
1 teaspoon salt
1 egg, well beaten

¾ cup orange juice
1 tablespoon grated orange rind
3 tablespoons cooking oil
½ cup chopped walnuts
2 cups fresh or frozen cranberries, coarsely chopped

Sift together flour, sugar, baking powder, soda, and salt. Combine separately egg, orange juice, orange rind, and cooking oil. Make a well in dry ingredients and add egg mixture all at once. Mix only to dampen. Fold in walnuts and cranberries. Spoon into greased loaf pan (9x5x3). Spread corners and sides slightly higher than center. Bake in oven at 350 degrees Fahrenheit for about one hour, or until crust is brown and inserted toothpick comes out clean. Remove from pan. Cool. Store overnight for easier slicing. Can be frozen.

*Cranberry bread recipe courtesy of the Long Beach Peninsula Visitor's Bureau.*

Spinach and Scallops Salad
1 pound Northwest scallops marinated in:
 ½ cup Johannisberg Riesling
 ½ juice of 1 lemon
 pinch of salt and white pepper
 1 clove garlic, mashed
 ¼ cup olive oil
After marinating at least one hour, skewer the scallops and grill
very hot until just done. Cool and set aside.

Salad dressing:
 ⅔ cup walnut oil
 ¼ cup raspberry vinegar
 1 tablespoon Dijon mustard
 1 tablespoon chopped shallots
 1 teaspoon chopped fresh tarragon
 ¼ cup cream
 salt and white pepper to taste

Blend all ingredients and adjust spices. Toss the scallops, one
bunch washed fresh spinach, and thinly sliced red onion with the
dressing and serve. Makes four servings.

Pretty—But Simple—Northwest Seafood Stew
3 tablespoons olive oil
1 large yellow onion, chopped
1 red pepper, diced
1 green pepper, diced
⅛ cup celery tops
1 fennel bulb, diced
6 cloves garlic, chopped fine
4 cups chopped Roma tomatoes
3 tablespoons chopped fresh basil
2 tablespoons chopped fresh marjoram
2 tablespoons chopped Italian parsley
½ cup Chateau Ste. Michelle Sauvignon Blanc
juice of ½ lemon
salt and pepper to taste

In a large pot, sauté the onions, red pepper, green pepper, and
fennel bulb in the olive oil until soft. Cover and cook over low
heat another 20 minutes. Add celery tops and garlic and sauté
until garlic is soft (five minutes). Add Roma tomatoes, basil,

marjoram, parsley, Chateau Ste. Michelle Sauvignon Blanc, lemon juice, and salt to taste. Simmer another 20 minutes.

Add to the sauce:
1 pound clams
2 pound mussels
6 crab legs cracked
$^1/_2$ pound white fish, such as halibut, cut into $^1/_2$" cubes

Cover and cook until shellfish opens—about 7 to 10 minutes. Serve as stew with crunchy Italian bread or over linguine. Wine suggestion: Chateau Ste. Michelle Sauvignon Blanc.

*Pretty But Simple Northwest Seafood Stew and Spinach and Scallops Salad recipes were created by John Sarich, Culinary Director, Chateau Ste. Michelle Winery, and are reprinted courtesy of Chateau Ste. Michelle Winery.*

---

## Grilled Marinated Washington Lamb
6 portions

Use barbecue or other grill.
Marinate meat and vegetables overnight, stirring several times:
  5 ounces per portion lamb sirloin sliced $^1/_2$" thick
  1 ea. red and green peppers cut in $^1/_2$" strips
  1 ea. onion cut in wedges
  2-3 ea. Japanese eggplant cut in rounds
  12 mushrooms

Marinade:

| | |
|---|---|
| 9 cloves garlic, crushed | 2 teaspoons salt |
| 1 tablespoon mint, chopped | $^1/_4$ cup balsamic vinegar |
| 3 tablespoons basil, chopped | 2 tablespoons lemon juice |
| 2 tablespoons black pepper, crushed | olive oil to cover |

Method:
  1. Pre-heat grill.
  2. Drain meat and vegetables well.
  3. Grill lamb and vegetables to desired doneness.
  4. Place marinade in sauce pan, bring to one boil, skim foam from top.
  5. Spoon marinade over meat and vegetables. Garnish with chopped parsley.

*Grilled Marinated Washington Lamb recipe created by Walter N. Bronowitz, Chef Instructor, Edmonds Community College.*

## Mile-High Apple Pie
12 servings

Mile-High Apple Pie

Pastry:
  2¼ cups unsifted all-purpose
    flour
  ½ teaspoon salt
  ½ cup vegetable shortening
  5 tablespoons butter, chilled
  4 to 5 tablespoons cold water

Apple Filling:
  12 Granny Smith apples, peeled,
    cored, and thinly sliced
  1 cup sugar
  2 teaspoons ground cinnamon
  ½ teaspoon ground nutmeg
  1 teaspoon vanilla extract

Butter-Pecan Crumb:
  1 cup unsifted all-purpose flour
  ⅓ cup sugar
  ¼ teaspoon salt
  ½ cup (1 stick) butter, softened
  ½ cup chopped pecans
  confectioner's sugar

1. Prepare pastry: In large bowl, combine flour and salt. Cut vegetable shortening and butter into flour mixture until coarsely blended. Gradually add water, stirring gently, until dough binds when pressed between fingers. Form dough into two balls, one slightly larger than the other, wrap, and refrigerate.

2. Make apple filling: In large pot, over medium-low heat, cover and cook apple slices, stirring occasionally until barely tender—about 10 minutes. Drain apple slices completely. Transfer to large bowl and add sugar, cinnamon, nutmeg, and vanilla; stir gently to blend. Set aside.

3. Prepare butter-pecan crumb: In medium-sized bowl, combine flour, sugar, and salt. Cut butter into flour mixture until coarsely blended. Add pecans and rub mixture briefly between fingers to form crumbs.

4. Heat oven to 400 degrees Fahrenheit. Roll out smaller piece of dough to an 11-inch round; transfer to 9-inch pie plate and line bottom and sides. Fill pie bottom with apple filling, mounding in center. Roll out larger piece of dough to a 12-inch round and transfer to top of pie, covering filling. Trim and pinch edges of bottom and top crusts.

5. Brush top crust lightly with water and gently press crumb topping to crust. Make several slits in top crust of pie to vent steam; bake 45 to 50 minutes or until crust is golden brown. Cool at least 25 minutes, sift confectioner's sugar over top, and serve.

*Mile-High Apple Pie recipe reprinted courtesy of the Washington Apple Commission.*

Yakima Valley Visitors & Convention Bureau

*The Yakima Valley and Tri-Cities areas are major wine-growing regions*

## From the Vine

Although Civil War veteran Lambert Evans started the first vineyard on Puget Sound in the 1870s, for years Washington produced only rough sweet wines and table grapes. The eastern section was too dry, and the western section was thought to be too wet, for wine grapes. Like most of Washington's agriculture, the development of viticulture parallels the history of the Columbia River irrigation project from the late 1930s through the 1950s.

### Came the Grape

Experimentation with wine grapes began in the 1930s, when Semillon vines from California were planted in the Columbia Gorge. While U.S. table wine sales increased steadily during the 1960s, by 1968 there were only about 400 acres of wine-producing grapes in all of Washington. Most of these were Muscat, Thompson Seedless, Alicante Bouschet, and Palomino. The late 1970s and early 1980s saw an explosion of vineyards producing Cabernet Sauvignon, Chardonnay, Chenin Blanc, Gerwurztraminer, Grenache, Lemberger, Merlot, Muscat Canelli, Pinot Noir, Riesling, Sauvignon Blanc, and Semillon.

By the 1990s Washington's 10,950 acres of wine grapes were second only to California in sales and attracted winemakers from California, England, Germany, and the former Soviet Union. State vintages had achieved international recognition and established reputations for their quality.

## It's the Climate

The effects of Northwest geography, climate, and soil combine to produce excellent grapes—the essential element of world-class wine. Washington's vineyards are located at the same northerly latitude of 46 degrees as France's great wine districts of Bordeaux and Burgundy. During the critical ripening period, extended daylight and crisp cool nights help grapes to achieve full ripeness, and produce wines with excellent sugar-acid balance and distinctive varietal character.

In Washington, wine grapes achieve maximum flavor at higher acid and lower sugar than they do in warmer climates. Sandy loam and volcanic soils give them their characteristic crispness and fruity quality. The result is the best of both worlds: Washington wines have more fruit than their European counterparts and more acidity than those from California.

The principal grape-growing regions—the Columbia, Yakima and Walla Walla Valleys—are situated east of the Cascade Mountains. With irrigation, growers can control vigor and produce wines that are aromatic and richly textured.

On the west side of the Cascades, Pacific Ocean air flow is aided by the warm Japanese current in moderating temperature extremes normally created by continental air masses. The temperate climate enhances the delicate flavors of cool-climate varieties such as Riesling and Pinot Noir. Here growers produce early-ripening varietals such as Chardonnay, Muller-Thurgau, Madeline Angevine, Siegerebbe, Gerwurztraminer, and other Germanic varietal crosses.

While some local wineries make single-vineyard wines, most prefer blends, mixing grapes with characteristics that complement each other. Approximately 70 percent of the wineries produce white wines and 30 percent market reds.

The Washington wine region is noted for its Bordeaux varieties of Cabernet Sauvignon, Merlot, Semillon, and Sauvignon Blanc. Johannisberg Rieslings and Chardonnays have been particularly popular. Full-bodied reds such as Cabernet Sauvignon and Merlots are immediately distinguished from those of other regions by their fruity taste, strong varietal character, and natural balance of acidity.

**Wine Festivals**

September–Grandview Grape Stomp

November– Thanksgiving in the Wine Country

November–In the Yakima Valley

## Sampling the Product

Most Washington wineries offer tastings and tours at select hours, days, and seasons. Many are small and visitors are sometimes greeted by the winemaker or principal owner. Out of courtesy, call ahead of arrival. The Washington Wine Com-

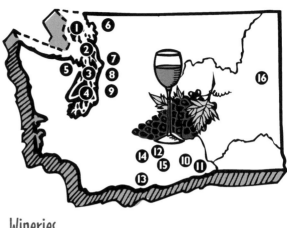

## Wineries

mission's *Touring the Washington Wine Country* directory offers a complete listing with addresses and telephone numbers. *FYI:* P.O. Box 61217, Seattle 98121; 206-728-2252.

**1) Lopez Island Vineyards:** This family-run winery produces organically grown wines from grapes selected for growing in the rain shadow of the Olympic Mountains. *FYI:* Rt. 2, Lopez Island; 360-468-3644.

**2) Whidbeys:** Loganberry liqueurs are a speciality. *FYI:* Wonn Road off Hwy. 525, Greenbank; 360-678-7700.

**3) Bainbridge Island Winery:** A ferry ride across Puget Sound and a short walk from the Winslow dock leads to a tasting room with an antique wine glass collection and European-style wines. *FYI:* 682 State Hwy. 305, Bainbridge Island; 206-842-9463.

**4) Hoodsport Winery:** Island Belle red varietal and a raspberry wine are specialties. *FYI:* N. 23501 Hwy. 101, Hoodsport; 360-877-9894.

**5) Camaraderie Cellars**: The winery offers views of the Olympic Mountains and tastings of Cabernet Sauvignon. *FYI:* 165 Benson Rd., Port Angeles; 360-452-4964.

**6) Mount Baker Vineyards:** You can taste Chardonnay, Pinot Noir, and Gewurztraminer while enjoying views of Mount Baker. *FYI:* 4298 Mount Baker Hwy., Deming; 360-592-2300.

**7) Silver Lake Winery:** This *Wine and Spirits* magazine "American Winery of the Year" winner makes hand-crafted varietals. *FYI:* 17616 15th Ave. SE #106B, Bothell; 206-485-2437.

**8) Chateau Ste. Michelle, Woodinville:** The cellar is located on the estate of a former timber baron, with a Victorian home and formal gardens. *FYI:* One Stimson Lane, Woodinville; 206-488-1133.

**9) Columbia Winery:** An industry leader for over 30 years in producing Cabernets, Merlots, and new varietals, this winery is housed in an elegant Victorian building. *FYI:* 14030 NE 145th, Woodinville; 206-488-2776.

**10) Bookwalter Winery:** Vintages include Cabernet Sauvignon, Chardonnay, Chenin Blanc, Merlot, and red table wines. *FYI:* 710 S. Windmill Road, Richland; 509-627-5000.

**11) Preston Premium Wines:** The list features major varietals, ports, proprietary blends, and sparkling wines. *FYI:* 502 E. Vineyard Drive, Pasco; 509-545-1990.

**12) Chateau Ste. Michelle, Grandview:** Washington's oldest continuously operating winery produces highly acclaimed Cabernet Sauvignons and Merlots. *FYI:* 205 W. 5th, Grandview; 509-882-3928.

**13) Columbia Cliffs Winery:** Basalt cliffs rising 400 feet give the winery its name and create an ideal micro-climate for its estate-bottled red wines. *FYI:* 8866 Hwy. 14, Wishram; 509-767-1100.

**14) Hinzerling Winery:** The Yakima Valley's oldest family-owned winery specializes in red and white table and dessert wines. *FYI:* 1520 Sheridan, Prosser; 509-786-2163.

**15) Yakima River Winery:** Founded in 1978, the winery is known for its barrel-aged red wines. *FYI:* Rt. 1, Box 1657, Prosser; 509-786-2805.

**16) Arbor Crest Winery:** At this winery, housed in a National Historic Landmark perched on a cliff 450 feet above the Spokane River, visitors can taste a variety of wines and stroll the landscaped flower and rock gardens. *FYI:* N. 4705 Fruithill Rd., Spokane; 509-927-9463.

*In addition to vineyards and a tasting room, Preston Winery offers a picnic area and a vintage farm equipment display*

# ART AND ARCHITECTURE

Tom Barr

*Seattle's Labor Day Bumbershoot Festival features entertainment for all ages*

## Performing Arts

Like the lush foliage which fills its landscape, performing arts and fine art thrive in Washington.

Seattle and Yakima's symphonies have received national recognition for excellence. You'll also find resident symphonies in Bellingham, Bremerton, Everett, Grays Harbor, Mount Vernon, Spokane, the Tri-Cities, and Vancouver. Selected cities offer opera and light opera, ballet and modern dance companies, community orchestras, chorales, philharmonics, and chamber orchestras.

It may surprise many to learn that Seattle ranks second only to New York City in the annual number of performances by local theater companies. There are at least 11 live theatrical companies in Seattle, including a repertory theatre, a Gilbert and Sullivan Society, a mime company, and the Fifth Avenue Theater, which hosts visiting Broadway productions.

Spokane Civic Theater and Interplayers Ensemble produce an annual series of stage plays. Tacoma supports several resident theatrical companies, and the Tacoma Dome and Pantages Theater host nationally recognized drama, dance, and comedy. Vancouver's Columbia Arts Center mounts a continuing schedule of live theater, dance, and music.

### Community Theaters
The Omak Performing Arts Center showcases music and theater in a state-of-the-art building, while Hoquiam offers local and professional

Centrum

*Bud Shank and other internationally known musicians are featured at Port Townsend's Jazz Festival*

performances in one of the oldest facilities in the west. Bellingham's Mount Baker Theater presents its local stage productions and motion pictures in a grand palace complete with a Wurlitzer 210 pipe organ and crystal chandeliers. Community and theater guilds also strut their stuff in the Tri-Cities, Othello, Gig Harbor, Grays Harbor, Anacortes, Edmonds, Everett, Port Orchard, and Bremerton.

Clubs and concerts rock and roll all week long, and the state continues to be a fertile ground for jazz and blues. Bud Shank, Julian Priester, Diane Schurr, and several other jazz musicians with international reputations live in Washington.

The high priest of the guitar, Jimi Hendrix, grew up in the Seattle area. Nirvana, Pearl Jam, Soundgarden, Alice in Chains, and other Seattle-based bands launched the "grunge" rock movement and spread its message worldwide.

### Festival Scene

Washington is also a hotbed of music festivals. Some of the largest include:

**Port Townsend:** Centrum Arts Organization presents concerts, festivals, and workshops throughout the year, with a varied menu of jazz, blues, fiddlers, classical music, theater groups, and a feature film conference.

**Bumbershoot:** One of the nation's top five festivals takes place at Seattle Center on Labor Day weekend, with over 500 performances on 20 stages, featuring blues, pop, and rock from Bonnie Rait and B.B. King to Fats Domino and Tony Bennett.

**Northwest Folklife Festival:** This major ethnic and traditional festival attracts over 200,000 people and 6,000 performers to Seattle Center each Memorial Day weekend.

**The Gorge at George:** This summer concert series in a natural amphitheater near the Columbia River features entertainers like Fleetwood Mac, Willie Nelson, and the Lollapalooza Rock Tour.

**Dixieland jazz** by regional bands fills the air at Hot Tunes Port Townsend, Long Beach's Ragtime Rhodie Dixieland Jazz Festival, the Wenatchee Jazz Festival, Friday Harbor's San Juan Island Goodtime Jazz Festival, and Ocean Shores Dixieland Jazz Festival.

**Classical music** is showcased at Spokane's Northwest Bach Festival, Lake Chelan's Bach Feste, Long Beach's Water Music Festival, and the Parnassus Chamber Music Festival in September.

*Seattle's* Troll under the Bridge

Tom Barr

## Public Art

Public art pops up in unexpected places in Washington. In addition to large cities, small towns, parks, and plazas, you'll find it gracing central Washington's cliffs, sidewalks, beaches, and waterfronts, and in fire stations, public transportation tunnels, and county jails.

## A Little Bit Crazy

While most of it is serious and ranges from commemorative statues to modern abstracts, some pieces display a bit of whimsy. Sometimes the public adds its own trappings, as in Seattle's *Troll under the Bridge* crushing a Volkswagen bug, and *Waiting for the Interurban*, in which realistic figures of commuters are often bedecked with shawls and handkerchiefs. They are among 256 public arts sites covered in *A Directory of Seattle's Public Art*, available from the Seattle Arts Commission. *FYI:* 206-684-7171.

In Ellensburg a full-sized sculpture of a bull reclining on a park bench is a favorite of children. *Dick and Jane's Spot*, nearby, offers a unique, eye-filling arrangement of disparate ingredients. At Central Washington University, also in Ellensburg, one of the sculptures scattered throughout the 350-acre campus appears to change shape as viewers pass it.

In Bellingham, the outdoor sculpture collection at Western Washington University features 20 works by major international, national, and regional artists. Tour brochures and audiophone tours are available at the campus Visitor Center. *FYI:* Exit 252 off I-5; 360-676-3963.

Off Interstate 90, east of Vantage, sculptor David Govedare filled a scenic viewpoint with a dozen horses running out of a large basket in a work called *Grandfather Cuts Loose the Ponies.*

*Western Washington University's outdoor sculpture collection displays works from major artists*

Bellingham Convention and Visitors Bureau

# City Murals

Several years ago, someone decided that exterior walls of commercial buildings would be a lot more interesting if they were covered by murals. Communities with public mural collections include Raymond, South Bend, Aberdeen, Hoquiam, Montesano, Ocean Shores, Westport, Ilwaco, Long Beach, Centralia, and Port Orchard. In Anacortes only four of 50 murals

*A Long Beach mural depicts oyster harvesting at the turn of the century*

are painted; the rest were reproduced from enlarged photographs, cut out of plywood, painted, and fastened to walls.

Toppenish's mural program has garnered national publicity and prestigious state awards for tourism and for art. Some of its 29 murals are over 100 feet long, and as in most cities, they depict local and regional history. All are painted by professional artists. On the first Saturday in June, Toppenish hosts a Mural-in-a-Day program in which approximately a dozen artists join forces to complete a painting in eight hours or less.

*Totem poles are found in downtown parks and on Indian reservations*

## Totem Poles

Native Americans along the Northwest Coast were renowned wood carvers who created highly decorated wooden masks and bowls. Each tribal group had distinctive styles and designs, which they used to portray supernatural beings in animal, monster, or human form.

Totem poles soar on Indian reservations and in metropolitan plazas, in state and city parks, and beside businesses. They depict legends or family heritage.

**The Museum of Native American Cultures** contains comprehensive collections of Indian art and artifacts from Indians of North, Central, and South America. The art gallery features 19th and 20th century Western art and sculpture. *FYI:* 200 E. Cataldo, Spokane; 509-326-4550.

## Fine Art

Fine art is never far away in Washington. You can find artists at work and displaying their wares from the pastoral San Juan Islands to the rugged gorges of the Columbia River and Hell's Canyon.

Port Townsend is home to potters, poets, sculptors, weavers, jewelry designers, and painters. On Whidbey and Bainbridge Islands you'll see resident artists displaying everything from weaving and pottery to fine art. After painter Morris Graves came to La Conner in 1937, others followed, and today this small town of historic buildings provides inspiration for numerous painters, writers, potters, and sculptors.

Seattle and Tacoma feature Thursday Art Walks, when galleries remain open late in the evening to introduce new exhibitions. Bellingham hosts a quarterly Gallery Walk. Olympic West Arttrek, a driving tour from Forks to Cape Flattery and communities along Highway 101, highlights 27 studios and galleries specializing in antiques, arts, crafts, and pottery.

*Maryhill Museum of Art sits on the edge of the Columbia River Gorge, seemingly in the middle of nowhere*

Tom Barr

*FYI:* Forks Chamber of Commerce; 800-44-FORKS.

### Art Museums

**Seattle Art Museum:** The museum is internationally famous for collections of Northwest coast Native American, Asian, African, and modern art. *FYI:* 100 University St.; 206-654-3100.

**Henry Art Gallery:** Nationally acclaimed exhibitions of contemporary and historical art are featured. Lectures, events, and children's programs complement each exhibition. *FYI:* University of Washington campus, NE 41st St. and 15th Ave., Seattle; 206-543-2280.

**Frye Art Museum:** Changing exhibits of contemporary art and a collection of 230 paintings from 1850-1900, representing 13 nations. *FYI:* 704 Terry Ave. at Cherry St., Seattle; 206-622-9250.

**Bellevue Art Museum:** Specializes in contemporary American, decorative, and regional art and traveling shows. *FYI:* 301 Bellevue Square; 206-454-3322.

**Tacoma Art Museum:** Permanent displays include Degas, Japanese Ukiyo-e woodblock prints, Imperial Chinese robes, and the only comprehensive collection of Dale Chihuly's glass sculptures in a public institution. *FYI:* 1123 Pacific Ave.; 206-272-4258.

**Maryhill Museum of Art:** This French chateau-style building is crammed with original Rodin sculptures, Fabergé eggs, Russian icons, chess sets, and the Northwest's largest collection of Indian baskets. *FYI:* Goldendale; 509-773-3733.

**Clymer Museum & Gallery:** A broad spectrum of styles and media from international artists are exhibited along with 80 *Saturday Evening Post* covers and fine art by Ellensburg's John Ford Clymer. *FYI:* 416 N. Pearl, Ellensburg; 509-962-6416.

**Whatcom Museum of History and Art:** Changing contemporary exhibits, Northwest art, and history are displayed. *FYI:* 121 Prospect St., Bellingham; 360-676-6981.

**Port Angeles Fine Arts Center:** Changing exhibits focus on contemporary art from established and emerging artists. *FYI:* 360-457-3532.

Bellingham Convention and Visitors Bureau

*Whatcom Museum of History and Art is the second-largest museum in the state*

Glass Art

The Pacific Northwest is considered the spiritual and geographic center of America's contemporary glass movement. Tacoma resident Dale Chihuly may be the world's best-known glass artist. His work has been presented in the Louvre, the Metropolitan Museum of Art, the Museum of Modern Art, and over 100 other museums worldwide. In 1992 he received the first National Living Treasure Award given in the United States. Pilchuck Glass School, which Chihuly founded near Stanwood, has been a catalyst for leading glassblowing artists and a model of education in the visual arts.

## Literary Washington

Washington has provided inspiration and residence for writers whose fiction and non-fiction have thrilled millions. Owen Wister wrote part of *The Virginian*—widely considered the first Western novel—while honeymooning in the Winthrop area. The late Ernest K. Gann of Friday Harbor won international acclaim with his best-sellers *The High and the Mighty*, *Masada*, *Fate Is the Hunter*, and other works.

*Another Roadside Attraction*, *Even Cowgirls Get the Blues*, *Jitterbug Perfume*, and other novels established Tom Robbins as one of America's foremost writers of innovative fiction. J.A. Jance incorporates many Seattle and Washington landmarks in her suspense and crime novels.

Leslie Rule

*Crime writer Ann Rule is a former Seattle policewoman*

Ann Rule, a former Seattle police-woman, is recognized as America's foremost true crime writer and an authority on serial killers. She has written over 1,400 articles and seven books on murder and gives seminars to law enforcement professionals on serial murder, sadistic sociopaths, and women who kill. Her best-sellers include *Small Sacrifices*, *If You Really Loved Me*, and *The Stranger Beside Me*.

### King of the Pulps

Frederick Faust, born in Seattle in 1892, was one of the most prolific writers who ever lived. Writing as Max Brand, Evan Evans, and under approximately 20 other pen names, he generated over 30 million words for pulp magazines and paperbacks. That's equivalent to over 530 volumes, or approximately one book every three weeks. His works covered virtually every fictional subject. He also wrote plays, motion picture scripts, and lyric and epic poetry. Faust's Dr. Kildare stories and the novel *Destry Rides Again* spawned several motion pictures and television series. Fifty years after he was killed at Anzio while serving as a World War II correspondent, his books remain popular and are reprinted in paperbacks.

# Filming Washington

Long before *Sleepless in Seattle,* Washington's scenery and cities had been immortalized on film. Clark Gable and Loretta Young traipsed through Mount Baker's snow in 1934's *Call of the Wild,* and later *The Deer Hunter* bagged his stag in the North Cascades. Robert Mitchum waited out the winter on Mount Rainier in *Track of the Cat;* Gary Cooper nearly swung from *The Hanging Tree* near Yakima; and Audie Murphy went *To Hell and Back* from Fort Lewis. *Benny & Joon* spent time in Spokane, Jack Nicholson visited the San Juan Islands in *Five Easy Pieces,* Richard Gere stopped at Bremerton for *An Officer and a Gentlemen,* and Robert DeNiro lived in Concrete in *This Boy's Life.*

The television series *Twin Peaks* turned the quiet communities of Snoqualmie and North Bend into major tourist attractions as visitors came seeking the cafe where agent Cooper found the "best cup of coffee" and the place where "cherry pies go to die." The community of Roslyn stands in for Alaska each week on *Northern Exposure.*

The prestigious Seattle International Film Festival, held in May and June, is considered among the five most important American film festivals. It screens more than 150 films from around the world and includes world premieres and work by first-time filmmakers. *FYI:* 206-324-9996.

*Spokane's Gonzaga University honors graduate Bing Crosby, born near Tacoma, with a statue and library containing his Oscar for* Going My Way *and other memorabilia*

Tom Barr

*The Washington State Convention and Trade Center is the nation's first conference facility to span a freeway*

## Architectural Innovation

Between 1945 and 1975 a style of architecture emerged in the Puget Sound area called Northwest Contemporary. It reflected influences of modernism, emphasized the extensive use of natural wood and glass to create natural panoramas from exterior scenery, and was used primarily in single-family houses, churches, and small office buildings. Since the style's popularity waned due to rising energy costs, architectural innovations have been few and limited largely to the Seattle area.

The Washington State Convention and Trade Center's unique style, characterized by harmony with the urban environment, has garnered national awards for architectural and engineering excellence, and innovative public or municipal facility design. The project includes a public park on top of Interstate 5, with fully accessible walkways for the physically challenged, leading to Seattle's city center. A glass-enclosed 30,000-square-foot grand lobby opens to sweeping views of downtown Seattle and Puget Sound. The center accommodates groups from 30 to 6,000 and is also used for concerts. *FYI:* 800 Convention Place; 206-447-5000.

The Seattle Art Museum has also received national recognition for its design. The five-story, 155,000-square-foot post-modern building is constructed of limestone scored with large-scale vertical fluting and accented by a colorful mix of pink sandstone arches, cut granite, marble, and richly hued terra cotta.

*The Seattle Art Museum and the* Hammering Man

Outside the museum, the *Hammering Man* swings his hammer four times a minute. The 48-foot black silhouette is one of several hammering men created by sculptor Jonathan Borofsky. Others are swinging away in Germany, Japan, Switzer-land, New York, Minneapolis, Los Angeles, and Washington, D.C.

One of the best places to see innovative architecture and public art is Seattle's bus tunnels. Each station has a unique design. The sculptures, murals, and laminated color transparencies on bus shelter windows represent a variety of cultures. After the city encouraged the participation of children and young people in creating some of the art, graffiti and glass breakage in the shelters decreased by 20 percent.

Seattle's Woodland Park Zoo is considered the founding place of ultra-realism in landscape design. The concept, introduced in 1967, emphasizes horticulture to hide fences and barriers and is now state-of-the-art around the world. At

*Animals roam together at Woodland Park Zoo, where barriers are hidden by foliage*

Woodland Park visitors can see elephants plodding through Asian tropical forests with over 30 species of bamboo and walk through a tropical rain forest with 23,000 plants. A northern trails exhibit, opening in the mid-1990s, features over 600 spruce, quaking aspen, birch, and willows as a habitat for south-central Alaskan animals. Visitors may watch bear catch a trout or pick berries from zoo bushes, and see elk, mountain goats, river otters, and bald eagles as they would look in the wild.

The natural environment has had a calming effect on both animals and visitors. After the zoo's naturalistic gorilla exhibit opened, battles between gorillas ceased; visitors stopped mocking the animals and began to speak in whispered voices.

*Bellingham's Fairhaven District houses fine restaurants, shops, and galleries*

# Historic Districts

Most of Washington's buildings were constructed within the last 125 years. Recognizing their beauty and historical significance, large and small communities alike have preserved homes and commercial buildings with attention to maintaining their original architectural design.

In Seattle, Victorian homes abound in the affluent Queen Anne Hill and Capitol Hill sections. Pioneer Square retains its historic flavor with beautifully detailed Romanesque facades on old-fashioned red-brick skyscrapers in a 20-square-block National Historic District with over 30 antique and craft galleries.

Tacoma has more than 100 stately mansions and homes, and Spokane's Brown's Addition also contains a fine collection of late 1800s and early 1900s residences. In Centralia, Victorian homes from 1865 to 1908 surround 1920s-era brick business buildings.

Other small communities with unique historic districts include:

**Coupeville:** This Whidbey Island town was founded in 1852 by Captain Thomas Coupe. His home, built in 1853, is one of Washington's oldest. A walking tour covers 28 buildings erected in the 1800s and early 1900s and an 1855 blockhouse. *FYI:* Central Whidbey Chamber of Commerce, Coupeville; 360-678-5434.

**La Conner:** The 130-year-old town is known for its picturesque 1890s homes and commercial buildings. *FYI:* 703 2nd St., La Conner Chamber of Commerce; 360-466-4778.

**Port Gamble:** Designated a National Historical Site, this town's architectural styles and traditions reflect the New England flavor of the 1850s. A country store built in 1853 is still serving the community. *FYI:* Country Store; 360-297-2623.

**Port Townsend:** With over 70 buildings on the National Register, this seaport exhibits some of the best examples of Victorian architecture north of San Francisco. *FYI:* Chamber of Commerce: 2722 Sims Way; 360-385-2722.

**Long Beach Peninsula:** Oysterville, founded in 1854, was a center for the early oyster industry and later a residential community. It contains many Victorian homes. Ocean Park, founded in 1883, displays a variety of building styles, including one home constructed of doors that were originally used in a pavilion at the 1905 Lewis and Clark Exposition. *FYI:* Long Beach Peninsula Visitors Bureau; 800-451-2542.

**Fort Vancouver:** The 21 homes along Officers' Row were built between 1849 and 1907 in Classical Revival, Second Empire, Italianate, Queen Anne, and Colonial Revival styles. *FYI:* 1301 Officers' Row, Vancouver; 360-693-3103.

**Dayton:** Eighty-three homes and five other buildings are on the

National Historic Register. The Italianate-style Columbia County Courthouse, completed in 1887, is the oldest courthouse in the state still in use for county government, and the Dayton Historical Depot, built 1881, is Washington's oldest remaining railroad station. *FYI:* Dayton Chamber of Commerce; 800-882-6299.

*One of the mansions along Officers' Row*

## Seeking Antiques

**Snohomish:** The Northwest's antique capital contains over 300 dealers in a four-block area and a historic district with 75 homes in Victorian Queen Anne, Craftsman Bungalow, English Cottage Revival, Colonial Revival, American Homestead, Dutch Colonial Revival, and American Foursquare styles. *FYI:* 360-568-2526.

**Port Orchard:** The community is known as "the Antique Capital of the Kitsap Peninsula." *FYI:* 360-876-3505.

*Snohomish is an antique lover's haven*

# THE SPORTING LIFE

*Bill Palmroth Collection*

*Community baseball teams have thrilled spectators since the turn of the century*

## Outdoor Playground

A variety of climates and terrain makes Washington a year-round outdoor playground for water- and land-based recreation.

### Spectator Sports

Spectator sports range from amateur and collegiate to professional teams. The Kingdome is the home field for both the American League's Seattle Mariners baseball team (206-628-3555) and the NFL Seahawks football team (206-827-9777). Seattle Center Coliseum and the Tacoma Dome host Seattle Supersonics NBA basketball (206-281-5850).

Spectators can watch tomorrow's stars play on real grass in the AA Northwest Baseball League at Bellingham, Everett, Spokane, and Yakima. Hockey fans root for the Seattle Thunderbirds at Seattle Center's Coliseum or Arena (206-728-9121); the Bellingham Ice Hawks at Whatcom Sports Arena (360-676-8090); the Tacoma Rockets at the Tacoma Dome (206-272-3663); the Tri-City Americans at Kennewick's Tri-Cities Coliseum (509-736-0606); and the Spokane Chiefs at Spokane Coliseum (509-328-0450).

Monroe, Port Angeles, Seattle, and Spokane offer auto racing through autumn. Yakima hosts winter horse racing from November through March.

### Golf

Come rain, sun, or snow, golf is an all-seasons sport in Washington. You can tee up on the shores of the ocean or Puget Sound, on an island, in moun-

*Apple Tree Partnership*

*Yakima's Apple Tree Golf Course's 17th hole offers the challenge of hitting an apple-shaped green surrounded by water, with a sand trap in the leaf*

tain foothills, or in dry desert. The PGA-rated course at Ocean Shores hosts the Pat Boone Classic and two LPGA tournaments, and the PGA Tradition makes an annual stop in the Seattle area. A course designed by Arnold Palmer is part of the world-class resort at Semiahmoo's Spit. *FYI:* 360-371-7005.

*The Ellensburg Rodeo attracts top national competitors*

### Rodeos

The Ellensburg Rodeo, held Labor Day weekend, is ranked among the top ten in America and includes a parade, country concert, and the Kittitas County Fair. Each August for over 60 years, Omak's Stampede and Suicide Race has featured top stars, a Native American encampment, and the suicide race in which cowboys ride at breakneck speed down a steep embankment and into a river. Other lesser known but equally exciting rodeos can be found throughout the state.

## Hunting

Deer, bear, goat, ducks, geese, chukkar, pheasants, elk, cougar, quail, and wild turkeys are fair game for hunters. The state's largest mule deer herd of over 17,000 roams the Methow Valley. Virtually every type of duck and goose in existence, and one of Washington's largest elk herds, congregate in the Yakima Valley.

Leavenworth and Darrington are prime mountain goat spots. The Potholes area near Moses Lake and the Tri-Cities are known for upland bird and waterfowl. Contact the Washington State Department of Wildlife for seasons and regulations. *FYI:* 600 Capital Way N., Olympia 98501-1091; 360-753-5700.

*The Yakima area is a winter habitat for Rocky Mountain elk*

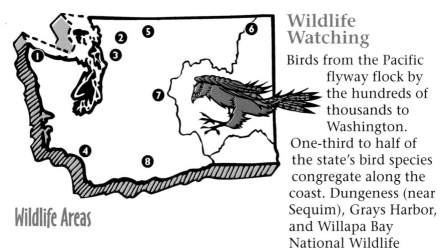

## Wildlife Areas

## Wildlife Watching

Birds from the Pacific flyway flock by the hundreds of thousands to Washington. One-third to half of the state's bird species congregate along the coast. Dungeness (near Sequim), Grays Harbor, and Willapa Bay National Wildlife Refuges rate among the best coastal bird watching areas. Beach walkers are also likely to see deer, raccoons, bears, harbor seals, sea lions, dolphins, and whales.

Other places which offer specific wildlife species include:

1) **Neah Bay:** Several hawks are among the 239 species of birds that have been sighted here.

2) **Skagit River**: A 1,500-acre sanctuary between the communities of Concrete and Marblemount protects the largest concentration of wintering bald eagles in the lower 48 states.

3) **Skagit River Wildlife Area:** Thousands of Siberian snow geese winter here near Mt. Vernon, along with 125,000 ducks and tundra swans.

4) **Julia Butler Hansen National Wildlife Refuge:** The refuge is a haven for Columbian white-tailed deer, elk, eagles, and ducks. *FYI:* Cathlamet; 360-795-3915.

5) **North-Central Washington:** The Columbia and Methow Rivers attract nesting loons, mergansers, wood ducks, mallards, canvas backs, Canadian geese, swans, great blue herons, bald eagles, and osprey.

6) **Flume Creek Mountain Goat Viewing Area:** This site in Washington's northeast tip is one of the best places to see mountain goats, bighorn sheep, moose, woodland caribou, and white-tailed deer. *FYI:* Metaline; 509-446-7500.

7) **Columbia National Wildlife Refuge:** A 22-mile scenic auto tour winds around ponds and marsh habitats for birds, coyotes, and other Channel Scabland animals, plus 25,000 wintering Canadian geese and ducks. *FYI:* Othello; 509-488-2668.

**8) Bickleton:** This small south-central Washington community is the world's bluebird capital. Hundreds of Blue Mountain and red-breasted western bluebirds gather here in the spring and fly to Mexico in the autumn.

## Recreation Areas

**Mount Baker National Recreation Area:** The summer hiking and fishing and winter sports area has a private resort with boat and motor rentals, RV hookups, cabins, and store. *FYI:* Baker Lake Highway; 360-856-5700.

**Coulee Dam National Recreation Area:** Grand Coulee Dam holds back the Columbia River, creating Roosevelt Lake. Over 30 species of fish inhabit the lake. Kokanee, walleye, small mouth bass, rainbow trout, perch, and sturgeon are the prime catches, with the best action coming in autumn. The 630 miles of shoreline along Washington's largest lake are popular with hikers and campers and

Roosevelt Lake Enterprises

are hunted for deer, elk, pheasant, and turkey. The world's largest laser light show and dam tours are available at Grand Coulee Dam. *FYI:* Coulee Dam Recreation Area; 509-633-9441.

**Lake Chelan Recreation Area:** At 2,486 feet, America's third-deepest lake thrusts its fjord-like grandeur for 55 miles into

*Houseboats are a popular means of exploring 130-mile-long Lake Roosevelt*

the eastern heart of the Cascade Mountains. Its glacier-carved granite cliffs and snow-covered mountains rise dramatically from azure blue waters. At the south end, Washington's premier full-service resort, Chelan, offers condominiums, hotels, and recreation ranging from biking, golfing, parasailing, hiking, snowmobiling, and hang gliding to water- and jet-skiing, kayaking, canoeing, tubing, houseboating, and paddleboating. It has more than a dozen boat-in campgrounds. At the north end, the Lake Chelan National Recreation Area at Stehekin sits in the mountains of the North Cascades. Stehekin, with about 75 year-round residents, offers campgrounds and trailheads for treks into the North Cascades. *FYI:* Chelan Chamber of Commerce; 800-4-CHELAN. Lake Chelan National Recreation Area; 360-856-5700.

# Water Recreation

Over 7,000 lakes and 208 reservoirs dot Washington's landscape. Some 4,000 streams collectively stretch over 50,000 miles. Counting the Pacific Ocean shoreline, bays, rivers, creeks, and off-shore islands, Washington's coastline totals 3,026 miles. With all that water and beaches, there are opportunities for virtually every kind of water recreation.

## Boating

One out of every five Washingtonians owns a boat. In some Puget Sound cities you can rent craft from canoes to fully-crewed yachts. On the west coast, Everett's marina is second in size only to California's Marina del Rey. Service facilities and moorage are available at Bellingham, Bremerton, Anacortes, Gig Harbor, Olympia, Port Townsend, Westport, Sequim's John Wayne Marina, and on inland waters at Vancouver, the Tri-Cities, and Clarkston.

*Fishing and boating have long been favorite Sunday outings for Washington residents*

Everett Public Library

## Canoeing and Kayaking

Kayaking is the most intimate and peaceful way to explore secluded coves, lakes, and streams. The Skykomish, Snake, and Yakima are popular rivers, and Seattle's Green Lake and Lake Union draw city kayakers. Near Sequim, Dungeness Bay and the Strait of Juan de Fuca's normally peaceful waters are excellent for sea kayaking. Surf kayakers often depart from La Push and Westport. At Ocean Shores canoeists can maneuver along forest shores and wildlife areas through 27 miles of spring-fed canals connecting three lakes. The University of Washington Arboretum rents canoes at the Waterfront Activities Center for use on Lake Washington. *FYI:* 206-543-2217. Northwest Outdoor Center offers kayak tours, classes, and rentals. *FYI:* 2100 Westlake Ave. N., Seattle; 206-281-9694.

## White Water/River Floats

April through June are prime months for white water rafting. Favored Cascade white water rivers are the Wenatchee, Skykomish, Skagit, Methow, Stehekin, and Suiattle. The White Salmon,

Klickitat, and Yakima Rivers are also popular, and once the spring run-off has ended, attract floaters as well. Unless you are experienced, avoid the Spokane and Tieton Rivers.

## Sailboarding

The Columbia River Gorge is a sailboarder's mecca. Over 200,000 a year flock to enjoy the ideal conditions created by the consistent 16-mile-per-hour winds and the river's downstream current. On the Gorge's Washington side, Bingen, White Salmon and Stevenson are sailboarding hot

*Sailboarders come from around the world to ride the winds at the Columbia River Gorge*

spots. Good sailboarding conditions also exist at Sequim's Dungeness Bay. *FYI:* Columbia River Gorge National Scenic Area, Hood River, Ore.; 503-386-2333.

## Surfing

Surfing is a year-round sport at Westport's Westhaven State Park. La Push's mile-long crescent beach is another popular spot. *FYI:* Forks Chamber of Commerce; 800-44-FORKS for La Push; Westport/ Grayland Chamber of Commerce; 800-345-6223.

## Scuba Diving

Washington has the third largest per capita diving population in United States. **Edmonds Underwater Park**, one of the nation's oldest underwater parks, and probably the most popular, includes 27 acres of tide and bottom lands which attract schools of fish and plant life. The Washington Scuba Alliance publishes a list of 68 diving sites and the activities and attractions which may be enjoyed at each, such as spear fishing, photography, and shipwrecks. *FYI:* 120 State Ave. Northeast #18, Olympia 98501-8212; 360-373-5367.

## Events

Columbia Cup Unlimited Hydroplane Races: In July the world's fastest hydroplanes compete on the Columbia River at the Tri-Cities.

## Fightin' Fish

When it comes to fishing and seafood, Washington has an abundance of both to challenge sportsmen and provide some of the planet's most delectable food. You might spend up to three hours landing a winter steelhead. Sturgeon from the Columbia, Cowlitz,

*At Kayak County Park, you can try for bottom fish from piers, boats, beaches, and jetties*

Chehalis, and Snake Rivers can weight up to 1,000 pounds. Halibut, which tip the scales anywhere from 20 to 300 pounds, have been known to break equipment, boats, and in some cases, arms and legs.

### Freshwater Fishing

Along with stocked rainbow trout, freshwater fishermen have a choice of five species of salmon, large- and small-mouth bass, plus

steelhead, cutthroat, German, brown, and Dolly Varden trout. Walleye, blue gill, perch, crappie, whitefish, sunfish, and catfish also inhabit many streams and lakes. Kelso and La Conner are known for their smelt runs.

### Saving the Salmon

In 1994 Washington responded to the worst forecasted salmon return in recent history by closing ocean salmon fishing and limiting it in other areas of the state. The reduced salmon fishing is likely to continue for several years. Check the *Salmon, Shellfish, Bottom Fish Sport Fishing Guide* published by the Washington Department of Fish and Wildlife for seasons and current regulations.

### Deep Sea Fishing

Neah Bay, at the mouth of the Strait of Juan de Fuca, is a natural crossroads for fish. Every fish swimming up and down the coast and in and out of Puget Sound passes Neah Bay, making it and its neighbor Sekiu prime deep sea fishing ports. Westport and Ilwaco are major deep sea charter centers.

### Bottom Fish

Ocean bottom fish, sometimes considered the bottom of the barrel, have their special attractions. They are big, readily available, and aggressive biters; they fight well and provide some of the best eating. With the exception of halibut, you can fish for them year-round from boats, shorelines, jetties, or piers. On Washington's coast you may land ling cod, sea bass, greenlings, cabezon, surf perch, starry flounder, halibut, and several species of rock fish.

*Mark Cedergreen, Westport Charters*

*The rewards of bottom fishing are usually a tough fight, large fish, and great taste*

### Shellfish

Gathering shellfish makes for a fine family outing. An average of 2.5 to 3 million clams are taken from Washington beaches each year. The best time to dig them is at low or minus tides. Three major Washington razor clamming areas are Long Beach, Twin Harbors, and the beach from Ocean Shores north to Moclips. Olympia, Shelton, Wallapa Bay and other clamming areas are thick with oysters. Westport Basin, Tokeland Peninsula, and Dungeness Bay are among the best crabbing spots. Species include Dungeness, Red Rock, and Geoduck, which can weigh up to seven pounds.

### Red Tide

Warmer weather promotes growth of Paralytic Shellfish Toxin (Red Tide), which affects clams and mussels. If eaten in sufficient quantities, shellfish contaminated by Red Tide may cause illness. The Red Tide Hotline (800-562-5632) contains daily information on areas affected by the toxin.

*Mount Shuksan, one of Washington's most photographed peaks, attracts experienced climbers*

# Land Recreation

National forests and parklands cover over one-third of Washington. Add Bureau of Land Management, state, and county parks, and several national recreation and wilderness areas, and you have virtually unlimited opportunities for camping, hiking, and mountain biking.

Rugged mountains, sheer cliffs, flatland desert, and variable winds also lend themselves to climbing and soaring through the sky. The Washington Trails Association publishes information on trails, road conditions, and hiking. *FYI:* 1305 4th Ave., Seattle 98101; 206-625-1367. Backcountry Horsemen of Washington is a source for horse trails and maps. *FYI:* P.O. Box 1727, Olympia 98507; 360-352-8979.

## Favorite Hikes

**Pacific Crest National Scenic Trail:** Washington's most spectacular hike follows the Cascade Mountains through national park and wilderness areas from the Canadian border to Oregon.

**Mount Rainier:** The 90-mile Wonderland Trail circles the mountain, through forested valleys to alpine regions.

**Olympic National Park:** Spectacular waterfalls frame the 13 miles into Enchanted Valley, a 5,000-foot-deep cirque with a 60-year-old chalet in a meadow at the bottom.

**Ozette-Cape Alava Trail:** The 9.3-mile round trip meanders through coastal forest to Cape Alava.

**Snake River National Recreation Trail:** The 16-mile, wheelchair-accessible trail connects parks and historic sites along the Snake and Clearwater Rivers.

## Ten Essentials

Washington weather, particularly in the mountains and at the seashore, is unpredictable. When hiking more than an hour away from your vehicle, take a compass, map, knife, candle-fire starter, waterproof matches, extra food, extra clothing, first aid kit, flashlight, and shelter.

## The High Country

Washington's most climbed mountains include Mounts Baker (206-775-9702), Rainier (360-569-2211), and St. Helens (360-247-5473). The Index and Leavenworth areas, Horsethief Lake (509-767-1159), and Peshastin Pinnacles State Parks (509-664-6373) are popular rock-climbing spots.

## Camping

Over 80 state parks have campgrounds. About 75 per cent have standard or tent sites. Backcountry camping permits are required in national parks. The Outdoor Recreation Information Center provides information on national forest and parkland recreational facilities, fees, and reservation procedures. *FYI:* 915 2nd Ave., Seattle 98174; 206-220-7450. National Forest Campground Reservations; 800-280-CAMP.

## Biking/Off Road Vehicles

More than 40,000 bikers ride through the San Juan Islands each year. The 69-mile Coastal Bicycle Loop travels to 1,500 feet through forested hills with views of harbors and beaches. A magnificent 50-mile ride through the Wenatchee National Forest connects Leavenworth and Lake Wenatchee. *FYI:* 509-662-4335. The *Washington Off Road Vehicle Guide* presents a comprehensive description of 35 ORV areas throughout the state. *FYI:*

*A group of 1900s bikers take a break along Puget Sound's driftwood-strewn beaches*

Everett Public Library

Interagency Committee for Outdoor Recreation, P.O. Box 40917, Tumwater 98504-0917; 360-753-7140.

## High Flyers

Lake Chelan, site of the 1994 Women's World Hang Gliding championships, attracts pilots from around the world. *FYI:* Chamber of Commerce; 800-4-CHELAN. Hot air balloons drift through the skies over the Snohomish Valley, Prosser, and the Walla Walla area. Seattle's Gasworks Park, Birch Bay, Ocean Shores, and the Long Beach Peninsula are popular kite-flying areas.

Tom Barr

*Washington's gentle winds and wide open spaces are conducive to hot air balloons*

## Alpine Skiing

Washington has 20 downhill ski areas. According to state ski experts, those with the top ten downhill runs are:

**Alpental/Ski Acres/Snoqualmie/Hyak:** The Northwest's largest night-skiing area is called The Pass. Alpental is noted for its vertical terrain and extensive backcountry skiing, and Ski Acres features the Northwest's steepest night skiing and terrain for all experience levels. Snoqualmie's wide-open runs are excellent for beginners, while Hyak offers a consistent vertical slope. *FYI:* I-90 at Snoqualmie Pass; 206-232-8182.

**Crystal Mountain Resort:** Ten chairlifts and a wide variety of terrain for novices and experts make this one of the state's favorite ski areas. *FYI:* Adjacent to Mount Rainier National Park; 360-663-2265.

Bellingham Convention & Visitors Bureau

*Mount Baker has been a popular skiing destination for generations*

**49 Degrees North:** Great powder skiing potential on 1,900 vertical feet and 23 major runs. *FYI:* Ten miles east of Chewelah; 509-935-6649.

**Mission Ridge:** Thirty-three runs from a 6,740-foot elevation afford panoramic views of the Columbia River Gorge, North Cascades, and Mount Rainier. Ski school, lodge, child care. *FYI:* 12 miles south of Wenatchee; 509-663-7631.

**Mount Baker:** This scenic resort usually has the earliest snow and the longest season. Its 1,000 acres of skiable terrain are rated 7 percent expert, 21 percent advanced, 42 percent intermediate, and 30 percent novice. *FYI:* 62 miles east of Bellingham; 360-734-6771.

**Mount Spokane:** Most of the 27 runs are rated intermediate or expert. *FYI:* 25 miles northeast of Spokane; 509-238-6281.

**Ski Bluewood:** This Blue Mountain facility with 23 major runs and 1,125 feet of vertical and groomed slopes has some of the state's driest snow. *FYI:* 22 miles south of Dayton; 509-382-4725.

**Silver Star Glacier:** The remote site offers Washington's only heli-skiing. *FYI:* 16 miles west of Winthrop; 800-494-HELI.

**Stevens Pass:** Six double chairlifts, two triple chairlifts, a lodge, and day and night skiing are situated at an elevation of 5,800 feet.

Bellingham Convention & Visitors Bureau

*Downhill skiers find plenty of fresh powder on Washington's slopes*

The 36 major runs, the longest of which is 6,047 feet, cover 1,125 acres. *FYI:* 37 miles west of Leavenworth; 206-634-1645. **White Pass:** This family-oriented facility features 14 major runs, 1,500 vertical feet, and 1-5 km. of groomed cross-country trails. *FYI:* On U.S. 12, 47 miles west of Yakima; 509-453-8731.

## Cross-Country Skiing

Popular destinations include the Colville National Forest, known for its consistent snow, high elevations, and excellent backcountry skiing; Mount St. Helens National Volcanic Monument; and Mount Rainier, with 126 km. of groomed and non-groomed trails.

## Snowmobiling

Seven national forests and a statewide snowmobile trail-grooming program provide over 80 cleared parking areas and 2,200 miles of trails through the Blue, Selkirk, Olympic, and Cascade Mountains. The Methow Valley, with approximately 150 miles of groomed trails, is a popular destination. Guides to groomed cross-country skiing and snowmobile trails are available from the Washington State Parks Winter Recreation Office; 360-586-0185.

### Events

**Ski to Sea Festival:** This seven-stage, 85-mile relay from Mount Baker to Bellingham Bay features cross-country and downhill skiing, canoeing, bicycling, running, and kayaking. May. *FYI:* Bellingham; 360-734-1330.

# SPIRIT OF WASHINGTON

In the century since Washington became a state, it has exploded into an eclectic place in which yesterday's history shares the land with today's aerospace technology and tomorrow's super-information highway. The spirit of Washington is an amalgamation of what has come before and discoveries that lie ahead.

In Washington, recharging the spirit inevitably means turning to the land and the water. Retreats are often as simple as a scenic afternoon drive or cruise, or a weekend getaway to a secluded beach for storm- or whale-watching. The spirit of Washington is also found in those special quiet places, a walk through an old ghost town, or celebrating unresolved mysteries.

## Healthy Soaks

**Sol Duc Hot Springs:** Legend has it that when the first resort hotel burned in 1916, wires short-circuited the organ, and it began playing Beethoven's "Funeral March." From late spring through early fall, today's visitors can enjoy kitchen cabins, a swimming pool, and three mineral water pools. *FYI:* Olympic National Park, 12 miles south of Hwy. 101; 360-327-3583.

**Olympic Hot Springs:** Soak at your own risk. These pools often fail water quality standards for public bathing, and temperatures vary from lukewarm to 138 degrees F. *FYI:* Olympic National Park; 360-452-0329

**Kennedy Hot Springs:** A 5.5-mile trail through the spectacular 576,865-acre Glacier Peak Wilderness leads to small undeveloped hot springs. *FYI:* Snoqualmie National Forest, Darrington Ranger Station; 360-436-1155.

**Carson Hot Mineral Springs:** Visitors can relax in mineral baths cooled from a natural 126 degrees, and stay in an 1897 hotel, 1920s cabins, or a hot tub suite. *FYI:* Carson; 509-427-8292.

**Soap Lake:** The Indians called it "healing water," and some claim it alleviates rheumatism, skin problems, and digestive disturbances. The alkaline water feels soapy, is saltier than the ocean and buoyant enough for floating, and is piped into several of the town's hotels and motels. *FYI:* Chamber of Commerce; 509-246-1821.

*Spectacular Rainbow Falls thunders out of the trees near Stehekin*

Tom Barr

## Special Places

**Stehekin:** No roads lead to Stehekin. Spectacular high country, some of America's most scenic hiking, bed and breakfast inns, cabins, a rustic lodge, and magnificent Rainbow Falls make it a popular day or weekend trip. The name means "the way through" and it is a good jumping-off spot for North Cascades wilderness visitors. Access is by boat, float plane, or hiking. *FYI:* Chelan Chamber of Commerce; 1-800-4-CHELAN. **Kalaloch Beaches:** This quiet stretch of the Olympic Peninsula offers a rugged shoreline dotted with sea stacks, lots of driftwood, magnificent sunsets, spectacular winter storm watching, and rustic cabins. *FYI:* Kalaloch Lodge, Forks; 360-962-2271.

## Washington Learning Experiences

You can learn about Washington in depth while combining travel with educational programs. **Sound Experience** offers educational sailings in Puget Sound aboard a 101-foot gaff-rigged tall ship built in 1913. *FYI:* Poulsbo; 360-697-6601. **Island Institute** conducts learning camps in the San Juan Islands on marine environment, scuba diving, and kayaking. *FYI:* Seattle; 206-938-0345. **North Cascades Institute** provides over 55 courses, most of them based at National Park or Forest Service campgrounds. *FYI:* Sedro Woolley; 360-856-5700. **Olympic Park Institute** programs include Lake Crescent cabin accommodations and 50 informal two-to-five-day classes on nature, arts, archaeology, and wildlife. *FYI:* Port Angeles; 360-928-3720.

# Riding the High Country

A favorite means of refreshing the spirit is to partake of Washington's magnificent scenery, either by car, boat, or train.

## National Forest Service Scenic Byways

**Mount Baker:** A steady climb of 24 miles on Washington Hwy. 542 from Baker Ranger Station through the Snoqualmie National Forest, past Mt. Shuksan and Mt. Baker Ski Resort, ends in the North Cascades at Artists Point.

**Mountain Loop:** This 15-mile drive on Washington Hwy. 92 from Granite Falls to Darrington follows the Sauk and Stillaguamish Rivers past Big Four Ice Caves and over Barlow Pass.

Tom Barr

*Snow-capped mountain peaks, ice caves, and roadside ponds decorate the Mountain Loop from Granite Falls to Darrington*

**Sherman Pass:** A 35-mile leg of Washington Hwy. 20 from Republic to Kettle Falls winds through Colville National Forest and crosses 5,575-foot Sherman Pass, the highest in the state.

**Stevens Pass:** Deception Falls, the rushing Tumwater River, and rugged Stevens Pass are along the 50-mile segment of U.S. Hwy. 2 from Skykomish to Leavenworth.

**White Pass:** A 50-mile stretch of U.S. Hwy. 12 from Packwood to Naches cuts through magnificent mountains along Rimrock Lake and the turbulent Tieton River.

### Cascade Loop

The 400-mile loop traverses Whidbey Island, Deception Pass State Park, Stevens Pass Scenic Byway, Lake Chelan, and central Washington's apple and cattle country. Climbing to over 5,000 feet, it cuts through North Cascades National Park and into a 90-mile stretch of unspoiled wilderness with no services.

## Riding the Rails

**Lake Whatcom Railway:** Early 1900s coaches and a 1926 Pullman car take you along the forested shores of Lake Whatcom. *FYI:* Wickersham; 360-595-2218.

**Puget Sound & Snoqualmie Valley Railroad:** Highlights include Cascade forests, Snoqualmie Falls, and historic Snoqualmie Depot. *FYI:* Snoqualmie; 206-746-4025.

**Mount Rainier Scenic Railroad:** Steam-powered trains with restored coaches and open cars wind through the forests of Mount Rainier's foothills. *FYI:* 360-569-2588.

## Ferry Ferry Popular

The nation's largest ferry system is Washington's top tourist attraction. Over 70 percent of ferry riders are recreational travelers out to explore the San Juan Islands, Puget Sound, Whidbey Island, and the Kitsap and Olympic Peninsulas. Most trips average 30 minutes, and the longest is three hours. The 23-boat fleet covers nine routes and transports over 18 million passengers and 7 million vehicles each year. *FYI:* Schedules and information; 800-843-3779.

> ### Ferry Trivia
> Ferry travel saves over 570 million miles of highway driving and over $190 million in vehicle costs per year. Ferry riders save enough fuel to run 64,000 cars for an entire year.

### Cruises

**Lake Chelan:** The scenic four-hour, 55-mile trip to Stehekin on the *Lady of the Lake* is among Washington's most popular cruises. *FYI:* 509-682-4584.

**Tillicum Village:** This four-hour outing features a traditional baked salmon dinner in a cedar longhouse-style building, an Indian legends stage show, and time to walk beach and forest trails. Blake Island was an Indian hunting grounds and the site of 1993's Asia Pacific Economic Cooperation (APEC) Conference. *FYI:* Piers 55 & 56, Seattle; 206-443-1244.

**Columbia/Snake River:** Cruise covers 1,000 miles of rivers and negotiates eight separate locks and dams. *FYI:* Alaska Sightseeing/Cruise West; 800-422-3568.

Tom Barr

*The* Lady of the Lake *approaches Stehekin on Lake Chelan*

## At the Water's Edge

### Lighthouses

More than two dozen lighthouses dot the shorelines of Washington's islands, peninsulas, and coasts. Most are operational. Ten are open to touring. Those that are easily accessible include:

**Whidbey Island:** Admiralty Head Lighthouse overlooks a scenic beach at Fort Casey State Park and is open for self-guided tours. *FYI:* 360-678-4519.

**Point-No-Point:** The site offers tours of the original 1878 station and panoramic views of Puget Sound. *FYI:* Hansville, Kitsap Peninsula; 360-638-2261.

**Westport:** Washington's tallest lighthouse stands 107 feet high, was built in 1898, and is operated automatically. *FYI:* 360-268-0121. A former Coast Guard Station nearby houses the Westport Maritime Museum. *FYI:* 2201 Westhaven Drive; 360-268-0078.

**Ilwaco:** The community at the mouth of the Columbia River has two lighthouses. North Head Lighthouse was built in 1898 and is located two miles west of town. In 1853 Cape Disappointment Lighthouse's construction was delayed when the ship carrying materials to build it sank just offshore. Completed in 1856, it is Washington's oldest lighthouse and stands three miles west of Ilwaco near Fort Canby State Park. *FYI:* 360-642-3078.

### Beachcombing

True beachcombers live for stormy days with strong westerly winds and high tides. After a storm or high winds, when jellyfish velella appear on the beach and wood or other debris floats ashore, it's likely that interesting flotsam and jetsam will soon follow. Japanese fishing floats—clear glass balls that are attached to nets to keep them from sinking—are most prized. Crab pot floats, green saki bottles, pieces of old ships, rope, and rolling pin-shaped floats often appear. Clallam Bay's waterfront and Rosario Beach are among the many fine beachcombing areas.

## Whale Watching

Every year between November and May an estimated 20,000 gray whales make a 12,000-mile round trip along the Washington coastline between Alaska's Bering Sea and the Gulf of Mexico. Many rest in the Grays Harbor and Westport areas, where a dozen charter companies offer whale-watching tours. *FYI:* Westport-Grayland Chamber of Commerce; 800-345-6223. Pods (groups) of orca whales that inhabit San Juan Island waters prompted the state to turn Lime Kiln State Park into the nation's first official whale-watch park. *FYI:* 360-378-2044. Whale-watching cruises operate from Friday Harbor, where orcas are central subjects in the world's only whale museum. Exhibits also cover other types of whales and marine life. *FYI:* Friday Harbor; 360-378-4710.

### Storm Watching

Winter storms are one of nature's great spectacles. As winds reach up to 70 miles per hour, giant waves continuously swell, surge into shore, crash against rocks, and fill the air with giant fans of white water and spray. In some communities storm-watching accounts for 40 to 50 percent of winter tourism. Some hotels have standing lists of guests to call when storms are approaching. The North and South jetties at Ocean Shores and South Jetty at Westport are popular beach-combing and storm- and whale-watching sites.

## Where the West Was Won

North-central Washington's Okanogan County has experienced virtually every type of Western history. It was settled by Indians, overland explorers, fur traders, missionaries, the military, homesteaders,

*Main Street, Winthrop*

Tom Barr

cattlemen, and railroad builders. It was also the setting for gunfights, cattle drives, gold rushes, and conflicts between Indians and whites, and cattlemen and sheepmen.

Winthrop retains a bit of the Old West's flavor, with some authentic 1890s buildings mingling with gussied-up false fronts and board sidewalks. *FYI:* Chamber of Commerce; 509-996-2125.

### Ghost Towns

Several near-ghost towns surround Oroville. A highland valley provides a picturesque site for Chesaw's aging log cabins and weather-worn buildings, country store, cafe, and about 30 residents. Old mines dot the Nighthawk area, and gold is still

mined at Republic. Loomis, an early 1870s cattle-raising center, remains a busy community with several historic buildings. *FYI:* Oroville Chamber of Commerce; 509-476-2739.

### Fighting Molsons

In 1905, the railroad's arrival created a temporary boom in the former mining camp of Molson. With land sales booming, no one bothered to file titles until homesteader John McDonald claimed the whole town. Angered by his action, many merchants moved a half-mile west and built New Molson. The two communities bickered back and forth for 20 years, tempering their animosity only in

1914, when they joined together to build a brick schoolhouse midway between them. Residents who had tired of the fight regrouped around the school, and Center Molson was born.

Remnants of the three towns include the original Molson bank, several residences at New Molson, and the schoolhouse museum. *FYI:* Oroville Chamber of Commerce; 509-476-2739.

Monte Cristo Discoveries of gold and silver 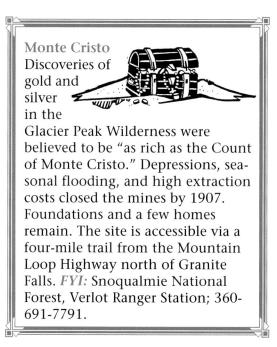 in the Glacier Peak Wilderness were believed to be "as rich as the Count of Monte Cristo." Depressions, seasonal flooding, and high extraction costs closed the mines by 1907. Foundations and a few homes remain. The site is accessible via a four-mile trail from the Mountain Loop Highway north of Granite Falls. *FYI:* Snoqualmie National Forest, Verlot Ranger Station; 360-691-7791.

Graves and Graveyards
Over 200 ships wrecked at the Columbia River's mouth earned it the title of "Graveyard of the Pacific." A map showing locations of 174 wrecks is available from the Long Beach Peninsula Visitors Bureau. None are visible. *FYI:* 800-451-2542.
**Roslyn Cemetery:** Twenty-six separate cemeteries clustered on a hillside reflect diverse nationalities, European customs, and artistry. *FYI:* Cle Elum Chamber of Commerce; 509-674-5958.
**Bruce Lee's Grave:** The martial arts film star is buried in Seattle's Lakeview Cemetery.
**Jimi Hendrix's Grave:** The legendary rock guitarist rests in Renton's Greenwood Cemetery.

Willie Keil's Grave
In 1845 Dr. Wilhelm Keil, the leader of a Missouri religious sect, convinced 250 followers to migrate to the Oregon Territory. He promised his 19-year-old son Willie that he would drive the lead team. Before they departed, Willie died of malaria. Keil placed his body in a lead-lined coffin, preserved it with whiskey, and put it in the lead wagon. It traveled the length of the Oregon Trail to Washington's Willapa Valley. *FYI:* Willie's grave overlooks Washington Hwy. 6 near Willapa.

# Unsolved Mysteries

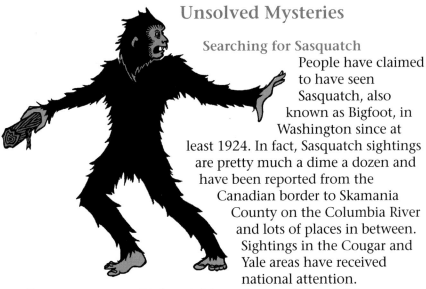

### Searching for Sasquatch

People have claimed to have seen Sasquatch, also known as Bigfoot, in Washington since at least 1924. In fact, Sasquatch sightings are pretty much a dime a dozen and have been reported from the Canadian border to Skamania County on the Columbia River and lots of places in between. Sightings in the Cougar and Yale areas have received national attention.

By most accounts Bigfoot is big and powerful, weighing over 500 pounds and standing six to eight feet high. The creature is covered with thick black hair, has a round human-like head, and stinks like rotten meat. No one has ever come up with a dead Sasquatch or even a skeleton. Many footprints have been found, but some have been proven fakes, so scientists remain unconvinced.

The Bigfoot Research Project in neighboring Hood River, Oregon, receives about 2,000 calls per month from people who think they've seen Bigfoot. About five per year prove credible. While the Project is not interested in bogus Bigfeet, call them at 800-BIGFOOT if you're certain you've seen a certified Sasquatch. Maple Falls' Bigfoot at Baker Festival pays homage to Sasquatch each June with a parade, Bigfoot look-alike contest, and storytelling. *FYI:* 360-671-4611. Carson calls its celebration the Bigfoot Daze Festival.

### Special Events
**Langley's Mystery Weekend**, held in February, is the oldest crime-solvers mystery event in the Puget Sound area. It features an array of suspicious characters who roam the streets, mixing with participants searching for clues to solve the bogus murder mystery. *FYI:* Langley Chamber of Commerce; 360-321-6765.

## Seattle Underground

One of Seattle's most popular tours features a fascinating walk, with humorous narration, through the former sewers and subterranean passageways of Pioneer Square. *FYI:* Bill Speidel's Underground Tours, 610 First Ave.; 206-682-4646.

## Cooper's Caper

On Nov. 24, 1971, a hijacker listed on the manifest as D.B. Cooper boarded a Northwest Airlines flight in Seattle. He demanded and got $200,000, then

*The streets beneath Pioneer Square are honeycombed with tunnels, storage areas, and passageways*

parachuted into the night somewhere in the southern Cascades, never to be heard from again. The search for Cooper and most of the money continues. Some of it was found by school children along the banks of the Columbia River. The small mountain community of Ariel is thought to be Cooper's most likely landing area. Cooper's Caper, held each November in Ariel, celebrates the event with skydivers, live entertainment, and a D.B. Cooper look-alike contest; *FYI:* 360-225-7126. P.S.: If you think you've seen D.B., call your local FBI office.

**Ye Olde Curiosity Shop** exhibits a number of nature's oddities and a couple of mummies. It also sells Indian and Eskimo artwork, ship models, Russian nesting dolls and lacquer boxes, Alaskan black diamond jewelry, and jade. *FYI:* Pier 54, Seattle; 206-682-5844.

## Star Gazing

Central Washington's Potholes area is excellent stargazing country. At Goldendale you can peer at the planets, moon, stars, and galaxies through an assortment of telescopes. *FYI:* Goldendale Observatory State Park Interpretive Center of Astronomy; 509-773-3141.

The Boeing Company

*Boeing's assembly plant in Everett is the world's largest building by volume. It covers 62 acres and is equivalent in area to 90 football fields.*

## One and Onlys

**Space Needle:** Seattle's most prominent landmark was built for the 1963 World's Fair. Its observation deck affords a 360-degree view of the city, Mount Rainier, the Cascade and Olympic Mountains, and Puget Sound. Two revolving restaurants and a lounge make it a favorite dining spot. *FYI:* 5th Ave. N. & Broad St., Seattle Center; 206-443-2100.

**Monorail:** The nation's first monorail was also constructed for the World's Fair and transports passengers from downtown Seattle 1.4 miles to Seattle Center in 90 seconds. *FYI:* 206-674-7200.

**North Cascades Smoke Jumper Base:** The base is considered the birthplace of smoke jumping. The first jumps were made in 1939 by parachuters into a wildfire to determine how to handle conditions fire fighters would face. Their successes led to other bases throughout the U.S. *FYI:* East Side Road, Twisp; 509-997-2031.

**American Hop Museum:** This one-of-a-kind museum features equipment, antique machinery, tools, baskets, and other memorabilia that tell the hop industry story over the last 200 years. *FYI:* 22 South B Street, Toppenish.

**Cape Flattery:** The cape is the northwestern-most corner of the continental United States.

Tom Barr

*Seattle's monorail crosses in front of the Space Needle en route from City Center to Seattle Center*

## Stonehenge

The full-sized replica of England's famous Stonehenge was built by Sam Hill as a tribute to Klickitat County servicemen who died in World War I. It was the first U.S. memorial to honor World War I dead. Hill believed the original Stonehenge had been used as a sacrificial site. He constructed the replica as a reminder that "humanity is still being sacrificed to the god of war." The altar stone was dedicated in 1918 and the structure was completed in 1929. Approximately 1650 tons of reinforced concrete were poured into wrinkled metal molds to give it the appearance of mortared rock.

## Who in Sam Hill Was Sam Hill?

Sam Hill was a lawyer, businessman, diplomat, and world traveler. He was also a Quaker, an eccentric, high-liver, apostle of peace, and a millionaire. In 1907 he bought 7,000 acres overlooking the Columbia River with the intention of establishing a Quaker agricultural community. Although he built a complete town, it failed to attract settlers

*Sam Hill*

Maryhill Museum of Art

and eventually withered away. At Maryhill he built a castle-like home for his wife and daughter, who were both named Mary. When neither wanted to live there, Hill turned it into the Maryhill Museum of Art. In Seattle, Hill constructed a large mansion to entertain the Belgian crown prince, who never came. He also designed and built the Peace Arch at Blaine. Hill died in 1931 and is buried inside a 14-ton granite crypt on a bluff 200 feet below the Stonehenge replica.

# KIDS' ADVENTURES

*Everett Public Library*

*Washington's beaches have been popular places for children's outings since the turn of the century*

## Kidding Around

**Woodland Park Zoo:** At Seattle's award-winning zoo you can walk through a rain forest and a five-acre African savanna with elephants, giraffes, lions, and zebras in a natural setting; visit a gorilla exhibit; and see over 50 endangered species. *FYI:* 5500 Phinney Ave. N.; 206-684-4800.

**Pacific Science Center:** Over 200 hands-on exhibits in five buildings explore mathematics, science, and technology, and also include life-sized dinosaurs, water works cannons, and a TechZone featuring virtual reality basketball, commercials, and robots. *FYI:* Seattle Center; 206-443-2001.

**Seattle Aquarium:** The many delights range from hands-on tide pools and sea otter families to rays, octopi, eels, and a Pacific coral reef. *FYI:* Pier 59, Waterfront Park; 206-386-4320.

**Omnidome Film Experience:** Soar into Mount St. Helens' crater by helicopter on a 180-degree domed screen and watch an actual eruption. *FYI:* Pier 59, Seattle; 206-622-1868.

**Seattle Children's Theater:** A variety of drama and entertainment is presented. *FYI:* Charlotte Martin Theatre, Seattle Center; 206-633-4567.

**Enchanted Village:** This amusement park features nursery rhyme characters, carnival rides, an aviary, and a petting zoo. *FYI:* Federal Way; 206-838-1700.

**Wild Waves:** Attractions include a 400-foot river ride, spiral water slides, rafts, and paddleboat rentals. *FYI:* Federal Way; 206-667-8000.

**Rosalie Whyel Museum of Doll Art:** Dolls, toys, miniatures, and teddy bears by master doll makers are displayed. *FYI:* 1116 108th Ave. N.E., Bellevue; 206-455-1116.

**Washington Zoological Park:** Over 60 species of threatened and endangered animals are represented. *FYI:* 19525 SE 54th St., Issaquah; 206-391-5508.

*Point Defiance Park's Never-Never Land*

**Point Defiance Park:** An award-winning zoo and aquarium exhibit sharks, beluga whales, red wolves, and apes. Never-Never Land, a life-sized replica of Fort Nisqually, Camp 6 steam train, gardens, and scenic shorelines are other attractions. *FYI:* Tacoma; 206-305-1000.

**Northwest Trek:** The 635-acre wildlife park features the largest natural outdoor exhibit of grizzly and black bear in any North American zoo, plus Roosevelt elk, bighorn sheep, and cougars. *FYI:* 11610 Trek Drive East, Eatonville; 800-433-TREK.

**Wolf Haven International:** The sanctuary presents a fascinating look at white tundra, buffalo, timber, and several other kinds of wolves, and also offers summer howl-ins. *FYI:* Tenino; 800-448-9653.

**Children's Museum of Tacoma:** A variety of hands-on exhibits and changing programs provide educational, fun learning experiences. *FYI:* 925 Court "C"; 206-627-2436.

**Deception Pass State Park:** The one-mile round-trip Bowman Bay/Rosario Beach Trail is a family favorite with thick forests, tide pools, and shoreline views. *FYI:* 360-675-2417.

**Olympic Game Farm:** Many of the tigers, white rhinos, grizzlies, and other animals have been featured in motion pictures and television shows. *FYI:* Sequim; 360-683-4295.

**Marine Science Center:** Living displays and fascinating touch tanks offer an exciting way to learn about Puget Sound marine environment. *FYI:* Poulsbo; 360-779-5549.

**Port Angeles for Kids:** A brochure produced by local students lists Hollywood Beach and Waterfront Trail as favorites because "there are rocks to climb and play on and there are places to build a fire and roast hot dogs and marshmallows." *FYI:* Port Angeles Chamber of Commerce and Visitor Center; 360-452-2363.

*Tacoma's Point Defiance Park Zoo*

**Touch Tank:** At a 1,200-gallon tank in Squalicum Harbor, children can reach in and touch starfish, sea cucumbers, anemones, and chitons. *FYI:* Bellingham; 360-676-2500.

**Chehalis River Wildlife Area:** A series of ponds along gently flowing creeks provide pleasant family canoe trips and fishing. *FYI:* Between Montesano and Elma.

**Cosmopolis and Ocean Shores:** These small coastal communities offer year-round fishing at ponds exclusively for children up to ages 14. (Children under 15 can fish for free in Washington.)

Tom Barr

*Spokane's Riverfront Park offers spacious lawns, rushing streams, and a large entertainment area with miniature golf and other activities*

**Riverfront Park:** An IMAX theater, carousel, and entertainment pavilion offer something for everyone. *FYI:* Spokane; 509-625-6600.

**Walk in the Wild Zoo:** This 240-acre park with a children's section is home to 200 animals from five continents. *FYI:* Ten miles east of Spokane on I-90; 509-924-7221.

**Three Rivers Children's Museum:** Traveling exhibitions, science and art, and computer games offer fun and educational entertainment. *FYI:* Kennewick; 509-783-6311.

---

## Events

**Children's Art Festival:** This July event includes entertainment and hands-on arts and crafts. *FYI:* Mount Vernon Chamber of Commerce; 360-428-8547.

**Sumas Junior Rodeo:** Several hundred youngsters rope and ride in this annual September event. *FYI:* Sumas; 360-988-5711.

**Seattle International Children's Festival:** In May, the largest children's festival in the U.S. presents performances from Japan, Canada, Columbia, Ghana, South Africa, Kenya, and the U.S. *FYI:* 206-684-7200

**Kids Learn To Ski Free:** In December, kids 5 to 15 can ski free at any ski area in Washington. Includes lesson, rentals, and beginner's lift ticket.

# INDEX